Body Work

Body Work

Beauty and Self-Image in American Culture

Debra L. Gimlin

UNIVERSITY OF CALIFORNIA PRESS

Berkeley   Los Angeles   London

University of California Press
Berkeley and Los Angeles, California

University of California Press, Ltd.
London, England

Chapter 1 of this book was previously published in the journal
Gender and Society 10.5 (October 1996): 505–26; and chapter 3
was originally published in *Qualitative Sociology* 23.1 (spring 2000):
77–98. Both are reprinted in revised form by permission.

Library of Congress Cataloging-in-Publication Data

Gimlin, Debra L.
   Body work : beauty and self-image in American culture /
Debra L. Gimlin
      p .   cm .
   Includes index.
   ISBN 0-520-21051-4 (cloth : alk. paper) — ISBN 0-520-22856-1
(pbk. : alk. paper)
      1. Beauty, personal—Social aspects—United States.   2. Beauty
culture—Social aspects—United States.   I. Title.

   HQ1220.U5 G56 2002
   306.4—dc21   2001027242

Manufactured in the United States of America
10   09   08   07   06   05   04   03   02
10   9   8   7   6   5   4   3   2   1

The paper used in this publication meets the minimum
requirements of ANSI/NISO Z39.48–1992 (R 1997)
(*Permanence of Paper*).

For Sven

CONTENTS

ACKNOWLEDGMENTS

Writing this book has been a labor of love and sorrow. Throughout the process, I have been fortunate to work with people who understood and supported my efforts, intellectually and emotionally. Central are the women who agreed to participate in the research, giving their time, offering their insights, and sharing their secrets. I thank them for their patience and generosity and hope that I have done justice to their stories.

I have also benefited greatly from the encouragement, advice, and generous collegiality of my dissertation adviser, Robert Zussman, whose thinking has guided much of this project and without whom it would not have been completed. Several faculty members of the sociology department at the State University of New York at Stony Brook also made significant contributions to the work, reading and commenting on numerous previous drafts and redirecting me when I lost my way. In particular, I thank Nilufer Isvan, Michael Kimmel, and Naomi Rosenthal. I owe a special debt as well to my fellow graduate students Lisa Handler,

Anna Linders, Megan Scott, Sharon Witherspoon, and Charlie Zicari for their warm enthusiasm, intellectual support, and friendship.

Finally, my family sustained me throughout the research and writing phases of this project. I thank my father, Darrell Gimlin, for his support and encouragement and my mother, Dixie Zacherl, for providing such a brilliant example of all the good things body work has to offer. Without the support of my husband, Sven Mattys, this book would never have seen publication. In addition to tirelessly proofreading and offering wise editorial advice, he endured hundreds of hours of discussion about the project and never failed to surprise me with his keen insight and sensitivity to the issues at hand.

Introduction
Body Work as Self Work

At nine o'clock on a summery Saturday morning on Long Island, New York, Pamela Swanson, the owner of Pamela's Hair Salon, readies her workstation for her first appointment of the day.[1] Pamela prepares dye, cleans several brushes, and sharpens a pair of scissors in anticipation of her first client, Rebecca Graham, a forty-eight-year-old grade school principal. Rebecca will have her hair colored a dark brown to camouflage its gray strands and then cut into a wispy, brushed-back style and blow-dried.

Two towns away, in his clinic, Dr. John Norris completes the only surgery he has scheduled for the day. In a fairly commonplace procedure, his patient, thirty-six-year-old Holly Marks, has had fatty tissue removed from her abdomen with liposuction. Not long after the operation Holly will return home, where she will recuperate for several days; John expects her to be enormously pleased with the outcome.

In the building across the street from John's clinic (and all over Long Island and the United States), women pack themselves into mirrored aerobics studios, where they strut and sweat for an hour or more to burn calories and tone muscles. Before these classes, they stand in front of full-length mirrors, trying discreetly to evaluate the bodies they have garbed in form-fitting Lycra outfits. And later that evening, at the Summer Fiesta of the National Association to Advance Fat Acceptance, nearly one hundred formally dressed fat women will drink, dance, and flirt with men who attend the organization's parties to interact with women who portray, for them, the ideal of female beauty.

Nearly four decades after the beginning of the most recent fitness craze, the popularity of body work shows few signs of letting up. Throughout the United States, women are lifting weights to build muscle; wrapping their bodies in seaweed to reduce water retention; jogging on athletic tracks, highways, and mountain trails; attending weekly weigh-ins at their local diet centers; and participating in any number of other activities intended to alter the appearance of their bodies. The increase in these activities has been cited as part of a "backlash" against women's social and economic accomplishments, interpreted as an attempt (largely male) to enslave them in preoccupation with their bodies and thus limit their capacity for further liberation. I do not share this interpretation. I find it implausible that the millions of women who engage in body work blindly submit to such control or choose to make their bodies physical manifestations of their own subordination. To be sure, women live under a system of gender oppression. Nonetheless, they manage to create space for personal liberation within those very activities that often appear socially and personally destructive. The processes operating within institutions set up to alter the female body are more complex than many critics acknowledge. Bodies are sexy, traditionally as objects of physical desire and more recently as subjects for social scientific concern. While historically the domain of anthropologists, the body has lately become an important focus of sociological attention. Today books and articles dealing with the body are multiplying rapidly in a number of academic fields.[2]

Because the body is arguably the location from which all social life begins, it is a logical starting point for sociological study. More important, though, the body is a medium of culture. It is the surface on which prevailing rules of a culture are written.[3] The shared attitudes and practices of social groups are played out at the level of the body, revealing cultural notions of distinctions based on age, sexual orientation, social class, gender, and ethnicity. But cultural rules are not only revealed through the body; they also shape the ways in which the body performs and appears. Ultimately, it is through the body's actions and demeanor that the self is constructed and displayed to the social world.

The self that is enacted through the body is both a social construction and, at least at the level of cultural understanding, a distinctively individual possession. In this sense, the body is one critical point at which the social meets the individual and from which a self is created. The body is fundamental to the self because it serves to indicate who an individual is internally, what habits the person has, and even what social value the individual merits. And the body is central to modern conceptions of gender. Components of the gender dichotomy as conceptualized in contemporary Western society—including strength and weakness, activity and passivity, sexuality and neutrality—are linked inseparably to the physical. The very "nature" of maleness or femaleness is intrinsically embodied.

While the body is important to the gender display of both men and women, it is particularly central to notions of femininity. Despite the advances of the feminist movement—or, perhaps, as Naomi Wolf has argued, because of them—women in modern society face particular and intense pressures to meet certain ideals of beauty. Physical attractiveness is simply more important for women than for men, a fact that contributes to women's preoccupation with appearance and psychological, physical, and financial investment in their bodies. Women, far more than men, involve themselves in groups aimed at altering the body. Women, far more than men, become victims of problematic relationships with their bodies, such as anorexia, bulimia, and compulsive overeating. Indeed, in a recent survey in the United States, a majority of women claimed that they fear dying less than they fear getting fat. It is unlikely that a woman living in contemporary Western society could ignore her physical appearance. If she did, she would be stigmatized as unfeminine or socially unaware. While men definitely face pressures to meet certain social ideals of masculinity, greater cultural variation is permitted in their physical bodies. Yet, although numerous writers and social commentators have argued that women face enormous pressures to match unattainable conceptualizations of beauty, few have empirically studied women's own interpretations of their participation in body work.[4]

Because men and women alike value women in accordance with their appearances, what women look like becomes symbolic of their characters—indeed, of their very selves. The link between the body and identity is more explicit among women because for them, more than for men, the body is a primary indicator of self to the outside world.[5] Some authors have argued that the beauty industry itself has fostered the link of body to self by urging women to use its products to create individuality. At the same time, the female identity is tainted by the fact that it is associated with and displayed through the female body—whether or not women themselves conceptualize the self and the body as united. With few exceptions, women are incapable of attaining the appearance idealized by contemporary culture.[6] Women's bodies are, therefore, by definition, violations of cultural imperatives.

Indeed, over the past few decades, the ideal female body has diverged more and more from the average North American woman's physical reality. In 1954, Miss America was 5'8" and weighed 132 pounds. Today, the average Miss America contestant stands 5'8" tall and weighs just 117 pounds. Only twenty-seven years ago, the typical fashion model weighed 8 percent less than the average American woman. In 1990, that difference had grown to 23 percent.[7] According to one source, the ideal female model today stands between 5'8" and 6' tall and weighs 125 pounds, whereas the average American woman stands 5'4" tall and weighs 140 pounds.[8] Furthermore, the average woman's body size has increased considerably over the past forty years; American women of the 1990s are considerably larger than those of the 1950s. Clearly, most women today have bodies that fall far short of the standard glamorized by our media and culture. And women's physical deficiencies (such as unruly hair, cellulite, wrinkled skin, or excess weight) have come increasingly to be viewed as evidence of moral weakness. The imperfect body has become a sign of an imperfect character.

Because most women can never achieve an ideal body, they must instead attempt to repair the flawed identities that imperfect bodies symbolize. Thus, I argue that body work is in fact work on the self. By engaging in body work, women are able to negotiate normative identities by diminishing their personal responsibility for a body that fails to meet cultural mandates. A long tradition in sociology has examined activities conceptually similar to those studied here—that is, activities intended to disavow deviance and to bestow on the actor an appearance of conformity. Through the concept of "vocabularies of motive," C. Wright Mills was the first to explain the processes through which norm breaking is explained and socially interpreted.[9] More recently, sociologists have focused on the techniques people use to improve presentations of self.[10] Still others have studied attempts to neutralize norm violation among various deviant groups, including the visually handicapped, rapists, child molesters, exotic dancers, hit men, and the divorced.[11] In each case, behaviors intended to neutralize the deviant meaning of certain acts imply knowledge of cultural rules and understandings, together with an effort to position behavior within the range of the normal.

In one example of this type of work, Marvin Scott and Stanford Lyman describe excuses and justifications—linguistic "accounts"—that explain and diminish blame for a socially unacceptable act.[12] Accounts, according to these authors, are socially approved vocabularies that neutralize an act or its consequences; they are also the manifestation of an underlying negotiation of selfhood. Though frequently employed, they are not always effective: individuals who participate in deviant acts do not always successfully renegotiate identity in their own eyes or in the perceptions of others. For instance, John P. Hewitt and Randall Stokes argue that one type of aligning action, called a "disclaimer," attempts to undermine the potentially negative meanings of intended behavior. Individuals use disclaimers to show that they expect disapproval and to thwart it by detaching identity from impending words or deeds.[13] For example, such statements as "What I'm going to say may sound rude" or "Don't overreact to what I'm about to tell you" imply that the speakers expect negative reactions to the statements, and they attempt to diminish disapproval by either detaching themselves from its object (i.e., the "rude" statement) or disparaging the reaction itself (here, by calling it an overreaction). A successful disclaimer may both protect identity and convince the listener that an opinion or deed is correct and moral.[14] However, the ability to renegotiate identity varies considerably with the severity of the norm violation, the context of the activity, and the social characteristics of the individuals involved.[15]

In the chapters that follow, I report on four settings in which women attempt to renegotiate identity by changing their bodies, their perceptions of their bodies, or both. Within these settings—a hair salon, aerobics classes, a plastic surgeon's office, and a social and political organization for fat people—I examine how women come to terms with the differences between their own bodies and ideal female beauty. I examine these settings not only as locations of work on the body but simultaneously as sites for constructing accounts of body and self.

Although my arguments are anchored in observation and evidence from women's lives, they originate from the theories and literatures of cultural studies, symbolic interactionism, and feminism. From cultural studies, in particular, I draw a concept of the body shaped not only by individual experience but also by the cultural meanings attached to embodiment.[16] However, I do not subscribe to the notion (inherent in the thinking of many social and literary critics) that these meanings take on a life of their own. Rather, I contend that meanings are embedded in institutions and negotiated—like identity itself—at the levels of the individual and the group.[17] Moreover, meanings attached to the body are created in part within institutions devoted to altering it. Inevitably, they are shaped by the women who occupy those institutions.[18]

While these literatures offer us a flexible and complex image of the body, they do little to help us explore empirically how women use the body to negotiate identity. They also fail to offer a sufficient theoretical foundation for beginning that exploration. Most important, they underestimate the role of individual and collective agency in the negotiation of women's understanding of their bodies and identities. From this literature it seems that the battle over meanings of self and body has ended, with the forces of misogyny victorious. Individuals, it would appear, have little power to react to either cultural or institutional forces. For example, Michel Foucault suggests that "power relations can materially penetrate the body in depth, without depending even on the mediation of the subject's own representations."[19] Such discussions position women as "recipients" of culture, incapable of questioning its imperatives or reacting to them. While I agree that power operates materially, I am unwilling to discount the potential for female mediation. It is a scholarly (and political) error to see women as no more than dupes of culture. Furthermore, to overlook the arenas in which meanings of the body are contested is to miss much of what is most important about contemporary body work. I argue instead that women—both individually and collectively—are capable (within limits) of transforming cultural meanings. And in so doing, women position and reposition themselves—consciously or not—in relation to contemporary ideologies of beauty.

My approach to the body is much more sociological than most other discussions of the topic. An image of the body shaped only by cultural meanings underemphasizes the role of social structure in the creation and maintenance of identity. The meanings of the body are neither free-floating in culture nor created solely by individuals, but are embedded in those institutions where culture and individual effort meet. Thus, group forces, commercial interests, professional considerations, and the structures of communities act, as fully as culture and individual negotiation do, to construct the relationship between self and body. A clear understanding of women's attempts to negotiate identity through work on the body requires an appreciation of both social structure and individual negotiation of culture. Therefore, I examine how individuals negotiate the relationship between body and self in the context of a social structure and culture that simultaneously provide resources for the creation of identities and place limits on those identities. I focus on the experiences of individuals, yet I insist that those experiences are shaped both by the cultural mandates of beauty ideology and by the collective processes of groups, organizations, and institutions.

BODY WORKERS

The data for this project are drawn from participant-observation in four settings of female body work: Pamela's Hair Salon, two aerobics classes, the office of a cosmetic surgeon, and meetings of the National Association to Advance Fat Acceptance (NAAFA). The women who inhabit these settings are attempting to change their appearances, or the meanings of their appearances, although they employ different methods for doing so.

I chose these settings because they represent a range of body work performed by contemporary women. Because I am interested in how work on the body is used to negotiate gendered identity, I look at its use specifically among individuals who have chosen to participate in these organizations, rather than, say, a random sampling of women who may participate in body work to varying degrees. While a generalizable sample might provide excellent information concerning national averages of, say, financial investment or time spent in body work, it would tell us little about the processes of identity negotiation carried out within institutions organized to alter the female body. My exploration of how beauty and health organizations provide both resources for and limitations on women's negotiation of identity focuses not on individuals alone, but rather on individuals within institutions.

Each setting represents different aspects of contemporary body work. Selected for their unique organizational structures and social class compositions, the sites encompass varying degrees of commercialization and different levels of financial, physical, and psychological investment. Plastic surgery and hairstyling are characterized by a dyadic organization, with one client or patient interacting almost exclusively with one beautician or surgeon, while the aerobics classes and NAAFA are organized so that members frequently interact with numerous others. As a result, women who participate in hairstyling and cosmetic surgery are more influenced by the opinions, advice, and techniques of a particular representative of beauty ideology than are members of aerobics classes or, even more markedly, NAAFA. Women in aerobics and NAAFA, on the other hand, rely more heavily on the attitudes of fellow group members toward beauty and self as they negotiate identity through body work. In these latter two groups, beauty ideology is transformed through group interaction. While the filtering processes of groups provide women with greater resources for resisting beauty ideology, these resources do not always allow them to construct positive notions of either self or body.

Furthermore, plastic surgery and hairstyling offer distinct images of the power relationship between the seller and buyer of beauty. The plastic surgeon occupies a higher social status (associated with gender, education, and professional position) than do most patients. Beauticians, however, have lower social status than their clients, and this disparity privileges the clients' class-based understandings of beauty and hair. Because customers assume that hairdressers fail to share their middle-class understandings of beauty, they reject both stylists' advice about appearance and their claims to expertise in contemporary notions of beauty. In sharp contrast, the cosmetic surgeon not only operates on patients but also has the power to deny them procedures for which the surgeon believes them to be psychologically or physically unfit. That is, independent of a woman's desire for or ability to afford cosmetic surgery, her surgeon ultimately decides if she "deserves" the procedure. For this reason as well as others, the cosmetic surgeon wields far greater influence over his clientele.

While both plastic surgery and hairstyling are organized around commercial interests, aerobics classes are commonly offered in not-for-profit settings. I chose to study two aerobics classes, one in a commercial environment (a gym) and the other in a noncommercial one (a university's employee wellness program).

NAAFA, too, operates on a not-for-profit basis. Unlike the other sites, this group explicitly rejects attempts to alter the body for the sake of appearance: instead, one of its primary goals is to construct notions of the ideal body that depart sharply from those recognized within the broader culture. NAAFA members reject the critical gaze of representatives of beauty ideology and the pressures that arise from the beauty industry's marketing efforts. Indeed, they are sometimes militant critics of contemporary beauty ideology. For these reasons, NAAFA provides an excellent opportunity for examining women's attempts to defy cultural imperatives as well as the limits placed on their efforts to negotiate normative identities despite deviant appearances.

My decision to look exclusively at female body work is based on a number of considerations. Women's body work offers the best location for studying the processes through which self and body are bound because the relationship between self and body is likely to be most problematic among women. While contemporary men must undoubtedly work to negotiate the relationship between body and self, women, more than men, face social pressures that make the negotiation difficult and complicated.

Studying only female body work clearly sacrifices answers to several important questions. I cannot make observations about gender differences in the relationship between body and self or examine how men resolve tensions between self and body through work on the body. Nor can I offer insight into men's management of the pressures they feel to conform to social ideals of physical masculinity. However, focusing on female body work allows me to examine the relationship between body and self where it is most critical.

While data from my research are not statistically generalizable, the organizations themselves are comparable to other sites for identity construction. The hair salon, aerobics classes, plastic surgery clinic, and NAAFA can all be characterized as organizations in which identity negotiation is carried out in specific ways. In particular, the issues of self-discipline and its ramifications for selfhood that are apparent in aerobics might also be present in, say, a weight-loss clinic or weight-training program, since these sites also emphasize willpower and perseverance. The hair salon, like clothing boutiques or cosmetics stores, speaks to issues of fashion and its part in displays of self. NAAFA aims to provide its members with a method for transforming identity in light of stigmatized appearances, as do groups for the physically handicapped and for racial and ethnic minorities. And plastic surgery speaks to issues of "passing," of altering appearance in ways that might be perceived by others as somehow deceptive, as in sex-reassignment procedures or the wearing of colored contact lenses.

I gathered data by taking part in the sites to the fullest extent possible. Some of the sites proved more difficult to study than others. For instance, whereas it was easy to sit in the hair salon and observe styling (with permission from the shop owner), I was not permitted to observe cosmetic surgery. And while I more or less "passed" as a member of the aerobics classes, I am too small in stature to blend in with the NAAFA membership. Yet by spending considerable time in all of the groups and by assisting the members in whatever ways I could, I believe that I was able to gain the participants' trust and, equally important, their honesty.

The length of my participation varied. I studied some sites intensively over short periods and others less frequently for longer periods. For example, I spent approximately four hours per week in Pamela's salon but conducted research there for only one year. In contrast, NAAFA functions are held approximately once every two months, so I participated in that group episodically for more than three years. My research in the aerobics classes was conducted over two and a half years, and my work in cosmetic surgery lasted two years.

In addition to the participant-observation, I interviewed twenty to twenty-five participants at each site. I gathered women's life histories with reference to their bodies, usually beginning the interview with the request, "Tell me about your body when you were a kid," and following the women through their lives, gathering information about their sentiments toward their bodies, their attempts to change them, and their own and others' reactions to those changes. The interviews also included questions focusing specifically on behavior associated with each site.

I found that most of the respondents participated in more than one form of body work. All of the research subjects had their hair styled. Two of the women in aerobics had undergone cosmetic surgery, as had one woman in the hair salon. Sixty percent of the women who had undergone cosmetic surgery also participated in some form of regular exercise, as did 15 percent of the members of NAAFA and 25 percent of the hairstyling clientele.

I began conducting interviews for this project in the spring of 1991, during my second year of graduate school. Never having come to terms with my own preoccupations with appearance, I had begun to search for sociological solutions to the discomfort that I, and many other women I knew, had experienced about our bodies. Specifically, these women described body work as a double-edged sword: while feeling enormous pressure to look a certain way, they also, as feminists, experienced tremendous guilt when they responded to these pressures through work on their bodies. I began my research as part of an effort to resolve this dilemma. When I talked with women in my campus aerobics class about their dissatisfaction with their bodies, I expected to find that body work served only to make them feel more deeply dissatisfied with their appearances. Instead I found that they were gaining unexpected benefits from their participation. I decided to test my findings in other arenas of body work.

I learned that arenas of body work provide women with the "socially approved vocabularies" that explain their failure to accomplish ideal beauty and thus serve to neutralize the flawed identity that an imperfect body implies in Western society.[20] At the same time, I saw that organizations, like culture itself, place limits on these negotiations. While women undeniably carve out a realm of liberation through their responses to beauty ideology, this liberation is limited by both culture and social structure.

The Hair Salon

Social Class, Power, and Ideal Beauty

"You have to let your clients know that this is what you do and you know best, or at least better than they do, what looks best on them," says Joanna, one of the beauticians at Pamela's Hair Salon, as she explains how she convinces her customers to accept her hairstyling advice. Joanna claims special knowledge of both fashion and styling techniques. She "knows best," she suggests, because she has immersed herself in beauty culture, better understands the current standards of beauty, and is committed to those standards. The hairstylist bridges the gap between those who pursue beauty and those who define it; she becomes the route to those standards and the means of embodying them in everyday life.

Many critics have argued that contemporary ideals of female beauty—and the work required to become ideally beautiful—have long-lasting and devastating effects on women.[1] Sensitive and compelling, these works incite outrage at the self-torture, deprivation, and mutilation women undergo as they attempt to attain hegemonic beauty ideals. Nevertheless, few of these writers provide empirical evidence on the everyday activities involved in beauty work. One typical argument posits that unreasonable beauty ideals have arisen as a backlash against women's economic and social accomplishments. They control women by preoccupying them with efforts to change their inadequate appearances and by draining them of self-esteem. Because standards for feminine beauty are inherently inconsistent and impossible to meet, women must struggle with bodies and appearances that inevitably fail to measure up.

Yet many women focus enormous energy on molding their bodies into the closest possible approximations of the female ideal. As they do so, they encounter representatives of commercialized beauty industries who help to shape both their appearances and their relationships to those appearances. Beauty workers like Joanna, because they are more fully embedded in and dependent on beauty culture than other women, play an essential role in the circulation of these cultural ideals. As representatives of the putatively hegemonic beauty ideology, with both a financial and personal commitment to that ideology, these beauty workers help to impose standards on women. But it is easy to overestimate the influence wielded by representatives of beauty industries, especially those who work on its front lines. Such an assumption positions women as "dupes of culture," unwilling or unable to respond to the pressures of beauty ideology. My research shows that this ideology (perhaps "ideologies" is a more accurate term)—at least in its everyday enactment in places like hair salons and aerobics studios—does not actually carry the enormous oppressive power with which it has been credited.

In this chapter I examine data gathered during fieldwork and interviewing at Pamela's, a hair salon on Long Island, New York.

Here I observed clients actively resisting the demands of beauty ideology (insofar as that ideology was mediated through hairstylists) without rejecting the larger cultural imperative for female adornment. While these clients do not question the notion that they should have their hair professionally styled, they resist their beauticians' conceptualization of female beauty by way of what Gresham Sykes and David Matza have called "appeals to higher loyalties."[2] Specifically, these women argue that their middle-class social status prohibits them from following the beauty suggestions of their hairstylists. Hair salon clientele deviate from norms for female beauty not because they reject those norms but because they accord precedence to the norms of another social group.

The clients' resistance is fueled both by their loyalties to middle-class professional society and by the very nature of the stylists' work. Beauticians are called on to bring an emotional component to their beauty work, to nurture their clients and, in this nurturing, to subjugate their professional expertise and knowledge to the clients' wishes. These emotional aspects of hairstyling, along with the commercial nature of the salon and the relatively low social and professional status attached to being a hairstylist, limit beauticians' influence over their customers.

Despite these limitations, the stylists at Pamela's are deeply invested in beauty culture and, as such, attempt to cultivate its ideals. As might reasonably be predicted from previous research in the field of gender and work,[3] the beauticians use hairstyling to construct gendered identities as well as to disseminate notions of ideal gender enactment to their customers. In so doing, beauticians attempt to position themselves as professionals with specialized knowledge and skills to nullify the real social differences between themselves and their customers.

Stylists' attempts to reduce status differences are, however, largely unsuccessful, primarily because of the emotion-laden aspects of hairstyling work itself. While beauty workers attach rich meanings to appearance and hair, these meanings typically diverge considerably from those of their customers, who use hairstyling to accomplish ends in keeping with their lifestyles. While both groups of women use beauty work to portray gender, hairstylists use beauty culture specifically to enact professional identities; their customers, conversely, use professional and social class identities to resist beauty ideology. The hair salon, as the institution in which meanings of hair and appearance are negotiated between stylist and customer, shapes these processes by simultaneously enabling and limiting women's ability to carve out spaces of autonomy.

RESEARCH AND METHODS

I chose to study a beauty salon because hairstyling is a form of beauty work widely available to contemporary women. The modern hair salon emerged in the United States in the 1860s, when wealthy New York women began to patronize Turkish baths. Popularized in part by the health reform movement, these baths became sites of luxury where women had their hair shampooed and styled.[4] Today, the beauty salon is still very much a "woman's place"; it has recently been estimated that one-third of American women go to a salon at least once a week.[5] Indeed, nearly half of every beauty industry dollar is spent there.[6]

From the critics' standpoint, hairstyling offers a temporary, superficial transformation of appearance within a commercial setting; it involves the purchase, rather than the achievement through some physical effort or sacrifice, of a style or image. Hair is a "nearly infinitely mutable adornment."[7] In fact, it can be styled to look different from one day to the next. And even though a hairstyle can be changed relatively easily, like clothing and makeup, it provides information about social class, ethnicity, age, and gender.[8] It also points to a person's notions of personality and self. Essentially, hair is a changeable, purchasable symbol of group and individual identity.

During one year, I spent over two hundred hours at Pamela's and conducted open-ended interviews with the owner, her staff (all New York State–certified hairstylists, and all women), and twenty women customers (90 percent of Pamela's clients are women). Pamela permitted me to walk around the salon, observing the stylists and customers and asking any questions I wished. Visiting at different times and days of the week, I recorded my observations of the relationships both between customers and stylists and among the stylists themselves. The women became so accustomed to my presence that often, in the midst of a conversation, they would call me over to the station, shouting, "You need to hear this!"

I found interview subjects by posting a small sign in the salon. Pamela helped enormously with this process by asking her clients to participate in the research, usually as they were finishing their procedures and getting ready to depart. For the most part, interviews were conducted in the salon waiting area, which was quiet enough for me to tape-record the conversations. The interview took different forms depending on whether the subject was a client, owner, or stylist. I asked Pamela and the stylists about their training, running the salon, interactions with clients, and their own appearances. I interviewed clients about their backgrounds and lifestyles (employment, education, age, marital status, partner's education, parental status, and so on), their hairstyles, their interactions with stylists, and the various forms of beauty work they performed. Customers ranged in age from twenty-one to sixty-one; most worked in professional occupations, and most were married with at least one child. While income and education varied considerably, the women were generally middle-class. All were white, either Western European or European American, as are most of the salon clientele. During my fieldwork, I never saw an African American client at the shop. This absence, although inarguably one of the limitations of my research, was not surprising, as this shop catered primarily to the white, middle-class community in which it was located.

I chose to study Pamela's rather than another salon because it seemed entirely unremarkable, little different from other salons I have visited in Long Island and other areas of the United States. It is located in one of the quaint older homes that make up the shopping district of a small, historical village on the eastern end of Long Island. It is decorated in a very modern style, with one main front room and one smaller back room. The larger room includes the receptionist's desk, a waiting area with contemporary sofas and tea- and coffeemakers, as well as sinks and seven workstations where hair is cut, permed, and blow-dried. Heavily mirrored and with large windows, the room has a bright, sunny atmosphere. Overall, the salon is tidy and friendly, warm and inviting. Almost everyone who walks in is greeted by the owner or the stylists, usually by first name. Salon services range in price from $10 to $100, depending on the work involved. Many of these processes take several hours.

Whereas Pamela's patrons are primarily middle-class and upper-middle-class white women, the stylists have educational backgrounds indicative of working-class or lower-middle-class status; at Pamela's, stylists too are white. The social differences between customers and beauticians allowed me to examine the unique and often divergent ways middle-class and working-class women use beauty culture to enact gendered identities.

This study would not have been possible in, for example, an upscale Manhattan salon in which stylists are considered artists rather than service workers. Such stylists would not need to construct professional identities as they do at Pamela's. Similarly, this study could not have been carried out in a salon in a working-class area in which stylists and clients might hold similar social positions. In both cases, differences in the way stylists and clients use beauty work in identity construction would be masked by their social-class equality. In contrast, the working-class stylists at Pamela's are neither artists nor their clients' social equals. Consequently, the beauticians use their employment (including their attachment to beauty culture) to nullify the status differences between themselves and their clientele. Finally, the racial homogeneity of Pamela's allowed me to focus specifically on class differences in relation to the "beauty myth."[9] That is, by studying a site made up only of white women, I effectively controlled for race and could therefore examine the independent effects of social class on the use of beauty ideology in the construction of gendered identities.[10]

Few of the women at Pamela's actually identify themselves as members of a particular class. Social class is, undoubtedly, a sociological construct, and, while useful, it neglects many of the complexities inherent in social identities. Most of the beauticians and customers I describe—like people in general—do not fit neatly into one social class. For example, Alice, a twenty-six-year-old beautician, attended a local university for two years and is married to a co-owner of a small drywall company. She wears her hair in a conservative shoulder-length cut that she bleaches to a medium blonde. Her clothing resembles that worn by many Long Island women in her age group; in the summertime, she typically dresses in knee-length shorts, loosely fitting pants, and skirts of varying lengths made of colorful cotton fabrics, with sandals or flat-heeled shoes. Alice speaks with an accent that suggests that she has lived on Long Island all her life. She uses makeup to emphasize her gamine facial features and tends to wear shades of pink, brown, and blue. Mandy, aged thirty-one, completed high school vocational training in hairdressing. Her father is a construction worker, as are her father-in-law and her husband. Petite, animated, and good-humored, Mandy has long, permed, and bleached-blonde hair. She dresses more casually than the other stylists at the salon, often wearing Gap or Levi's jeans, loosely fitting shirts, and sandals or sneakers. Mandy always chews gum and often calls her customers "hon"; she is also more likely than other members of the staff to compliment her clients on their appearance and skill with their hairstyles.

These women's choices about appearance and behavior involve not only employment, education, and income, but also taste.[11] Together with other traits, style and appearance preferences display a complex social identity that is both relevant for and shaped by class identity. Although I identify these beauticians as lower-middle-class or working-class women, it is obviously I, rather than the stylists, who impose these categories on them. The women at Pamela's did not describe themselves as members of the working class—or of any class for that matter— but they were aware of the status implications of their career. The women at Pamela's use beauty work to negotiate a social self. In that process, they also forge class identities.

THE STYLISTS

Cultural images of the hairdresser abound, so much so that the stylist has very nearly become a social type. The hairstylist played by Dolly Parton in *Steel Magnolias* is a frosted, painted, girdled icon of fabricated femininity who dispenses not only permanents and hair dye but also small-town gossip, marital advice, and tissues for her customers' tears. In *Grease,* the ridiculously coiffed "beauty school dropout" has an overzealous commitment to avant-garde beauty culture that alienates her even from other (less adamant) devotees of adornment. One finds frequent—and rarely flattering—images of women who immerse themselves in beauty culture and who attempt to bring the culture's practices and belief system to the lay masses.

The seven stylists employed at Pamela's salon neither consistently satisfy nor significantly deviate from this stereotype, though they are certainly devoted to the culture of beauty work. Most of the beauticians completed an academic program in high school, though some attended vocational school, where they learned hairstyling along with academic subjects. Alice attended two years of college. All but one stylist is married, and all those who are married have at least one child. Most of the stylists' husbands have blue-collar jobs (most work for construction companies), though the salon owner's husband is a barber who owns his own shop in a nearby town. The hairdressers range in age from twenty-four to forty-six years. All wear makeup and fashionable clothing, and all pay close attention to their own hairstyles and hair colors, which tend to change every few months.

The stylists are aware of the stereotype of beauticians. Most are able to describe the stereotype, though none believes that she conforms to it. Alice says, "There's a low-class image, and I know that I don't fit it. People say to me, 'You look like a teacher or a secretary. You don't look like a hairdresser.' In their own dumb way, I think they're trying to give me a compliment."

Alice considers hairstyling to be a respectable, desirable occupation rather than the "low-class" job of its stereotype. In fact, Alice and the other stylists are so committed to beauty culture that they conceptualize their occupation as a "calling." The stylists did not necessarily choose hairstyling; it chose them. As Pamela recalls, "I was cutting friends' hair in grade school. It wasn't something I really consciously decided to do. I just started doing it." Pamela simply had to be a stylist. Even so, after high school, she ignored her desire to style hair and worked temporarily as a secretary. And yet during the time Pamela was a clerical worker, she was still identified by others as a hairdresser. She says, "One day the boss comes over to me and says to me, 'Would you come in early Wednesday morning to do my hair?' ... I would meet her in the bathroom at 8:00. She said to me, 'My hair looks better when you do it than when I go to the salon to get it done.'" Others validated Pamela's calling even before she did, and eventually she changed careers. Danielle, too, says that she knew, at the age of thirteen, that she wanted to style hair for the rest of her life. Recalling that she enjoyed braiding other girls' hair when she was quite young, she observes that she felt compelled even in childhood to be a hairstylist. While hairdressing technique can be taught, every beautician I talked with argued that hairstyling talent is inborn rather than learned. Mandy explains, "It's one of those things, either you have it or you don't. You do get trained at school, but it's basically something you just know." The stylists believe that because they are "born with" their talent, they have a special gift for choosing hairstyles for their customers.

For these women, beauty (particularly as it is expressed through hairdressing) is not only one method of enacting femininity, it is the essence of femininity. Janet says, "A woman can't really feel good, can't really feel attractive or feminine, if her hair doesn't look styled, no matter what else she's got going for her." And well-managed hair does not occur naturally, but must be acquired through work. Thus Janet does not refer to the importance of "beautiful" or "healthy" hair, but instead stresses the significance of "styled" hair. Danielle pushes this position even further, arguing that "hair makes the woman." In effect, womanhood itself, as much as female beauty, is created through hairstyling.

The beauticians invest not only their conceptions of femininity but also their daily activities and livelihood in beauty work. Furthermore, they are the teachers and masters of their "faith," responsible for providing their clients with the appropriate instruction and instilling in them the proper degree of commitment. Nevertheless, while these priestesses of beauty may consider themselves the vanguardists, they occupy a distinctively lower social status than the novices. And their inferior status results not from vows of poverty or self-sacrifice, but instead from their educational and socioeconomic backgrounds and the cultural images attached to their occupation. The social hierarchy that grants hairstylists a lower status than their clients threatens beauticians' dominance in their own sphere. In the same way that a secular hierarchy (one that values financial wealth over spiritual purity) endangers a priest's influence on a congregation, conventional status distinctions threaten hairstylists' authority within the hair salon. Counter to the arguments made by writers such as Naomi Wolf and Nancy Baker, outside the hair salon, beauty does not reign supreme.[12]

To nullify status differences between themselves and their clients, stylists emphasize their special knowledge of gendered areas of information, including women's fashion, beauty, and style. They also perform "emotion work," or work that "affirms, enhances, and celebrates the well-being" of their clients, by positioning themselves as customers' friends, confidantes, and therapists.[13] The traditional criteria for an occupation to be considered a "profession" include extensive training, entry by examination for licensure, exclusionary associations, and a formal code of ethics. Hairstylists must be state-licensed to work in a reputable salon like Pamela's. In New York, certification requires 1,200 hours of training in a certified beauty school and written and practical exams. The written exam covers topics ranging from cutting and coloring technique to health and hygiene. In the practical test, stylists are required to cut, color, perm, and style the hair of live models. In many ways, hairdressing indeed meets the formal criteria of a profession.[14] Nevertheless, because of the negative stereotype attached to the occupation, its status is open to debate.

During their interactions with clients, the beauticians try to position themselves as experts, thereby reducing the status dif-

ferences between themselves and their clientele—who are, more
often than not, professional women. For example, Joanna says,
"You get the client who shows you something in a picture that's
nothing like her hair and you tell her, 'Look at the color, the texture, and the curl; it's nothing like your hair.'" Joanna's expert
knowledge about the suitability of a style for a particular kind of
hair is unavailable to the lay masses. In a somewhat different
scenario, Mandy explains that the hairstyle her customer
wants—long and straight in the back with short, brushed-back
bangs—is "out of date." She tells the customer to wear her hair
shoulder-length, with longer bangs on her forehead. Here the
stylist is making an argument about fashion, asserting perhaps
not special, but at least superior, knowledge of trends in female
beauty. Both strategies position the hairstylist above her client in
the hierarchy of beauty culture.

Although I have differentiated fashion and technique, beauticians seldom do so. Hair that is styled with technical competence and hair that is trendy become indistinguishable when stylists advise customers; when they equate fashion and technique,
the beauticians effectively broaden their area of expertise. They
are experts not only in hairdressing, but also in style, contemporary trends, and general attractiveness. Trish talks about making
recommendations to her customers: "I'll tell [clients] what they're
doing wrong and how they can do it right. People don't know
how to scrunch their hair. People are amazed at how much curl
you can get out of their hair when it's done the right way."

Trish is making both a technical claim about styling hair and
a fashion claim about how the hair should look when it is fashioned properly. In a similar example, Alice tells me that she suggests that clients with wide faces don't wear their hair "too short

near the jaw so their cheeks look bigger." While she regards her comment as technical advice about face and hair shape, it is clearly grounded in the assumption that wide faces are unattractive. Again, technique and opinion seem to be, if not the same thing, at least vaguely differentiated. Joanna tries to convince a customer "to color her gray," confiding to me that the client has "no idea how badly she needs it." While it is unclear exactly why the woman "needs" to color her gray hair—perhaps because she will look younger or the coloring process will make her hair more manageable—Joanna clearly assumes that she has knowledge that the client does not.

Hairstylists also attempt to nullify status differences by conceptualizing an alternative hierarchy. This hierarchy is not based on education, occupation, or income, but rather on appearance, manifest in the ability to choose an attractive haircut for oneself and to style hair competently. For example, Nancy comments, "You see these women who have a ton of money who don't know how to do their hair. I try to teach them how, but sometimes, oh, it's hopeless!" Implicit in this statement is, first, the recognition of a hierarchy that privileges income over ability to style hair, and second, a replacement of that hierarchy with one that positions the hairstylist as a teacher. Benevolent as Nancy may be, her attempts are often frustrated by her clients' ineptitude, independent of their having "a ton of money" or desirable social position. Moreover, the clients' inability reinforces beauticians' dominant position in the hierarchy of beauty culture. As the leaders of their faith, responsible for their followers' well-being, stylists accept control over their customers' appearances. Danielle explains, "A lot of the time, they want you to tell them what to do with their hair. They really don't know what will look best, so I help them."

Again, the stylists are not just leaders; they are benevolent, self-sacrificing leaders.

They are also counselors. Even though the salon interaction centers on payment for a service, hairstylists suggest that their associations with customers extend beyond the financial transactions.[15] The beauticians foster personal relationships with their clients by listening to accounts of their lives and displaying emotional attachment to them, evidenced through interest in these details, careful guarding of their clients' secrets, and concern for their well-being (especially insofar as "wellness" is conveyed through appearance). For example, stylists claim to be comfortable with the often intimate information shared by their clients. Pamela says, "I don't have any problem at all with anything they tell me, even if they tell me they're having an affair with somebody else who I do their hair, and the other one's married to another one, because they know what they tell me doesn't go any further. It's safe."

Because the information is "safe," as it would be with a trusted confidante, the relationships between Pamela and her clients take on at least one important quality of friendship. Although these relationships lack many of the features—such as socializing together outside the salon, visiting each others' homes, or talking on the telephone—that one would typically associate with friendship, having her clients' trust allows Pamela to see herself as their friend. Client-stylist relationships like this often develop over several years. The stylists seem proud of the durability of the relationships and pleased with their ability to provide their clients with a confidante, both because they express gratification in their role as "nurturers" (in things emotional and beauty-related) and because friends are, by common understanding, equals. Indeed, although numerous researchers have examined the negative effects of emotion work,[16] these stylists use the emotional component of their work to imagine themselves the social equals of the women they serve. They claim to enjoy learning about and remembering the details of clients' lives, making them feel important, and providing them with emotional comfort. Joanna says, "My people get blown away. I'm like, 'Whatever happened with that vacation you were going on?' ... They're important to you, and so you remember. It makes them feel nice. It makes them feel, 'Wow, she really listens to me.' They want to talk about their problems."

In considering their clients to be long-term friends and equals, the stylists see their customers as similar to them in bearing and personality. Alice explains that her clients are "kind of like" her in that they have "similar personalities." Like Alice, they are "young women" who are "going through the same kinds of things I'm going through." Alice sees her clients as similar to herself in personality, age, gender, and lifestyle, even though she is vague about the "kinds of things" that they are going through. In effect, she suggests that she and her clients live analogous lives and, by implication, that they are social equals.

Overall, seeing their clients as friends strengthens the stylists' commitment to their role in beauty culture. They believe that they are genuinely helping their clients—people whom they value and who value them. Nancy explains, "I just really love what I do. You see the results before your eyes. You make a suggestion and the client is really happy. It's just become a great part of my life." Nancy reaffirms her commitment to beauty culture, in this case, because she treasures her influence on her clients/friends.

Although the emotion work performed by stylists allows them to imagine themselves their clients' social equals, it simultaneously undermines the beauticians' claims to professional status. This paradox is evident in the many instances when beauticians cut hair in a requested style that they think is unattractive, ugly, or unfashionable. Hairdressers provide these styles because, first, they are financially dependent on their clients' satisfaction, and, second, they claim to be genuinely concerned with their customers' needs. However, even while they provide these "inappropriate" styles, beauticians deny responsibility for them by blaming them on their customers' poor taste. Janet says, "The woman that just left, her hair was so thin and dry, she really shouldn't wear it straight and long. She doesn't know, though … I wasn't happy with the style, but I guess she liked it." Related to her claims to professionalism and special knowledge, Janet is making a statement about the superiority of her own taste. Janet says that the client "doesn't know" how to wear her hair, but she fails to provide evidence for her opinion. She merely implies there is a "right" way for the woman to wear her hair that the client fails to recognize. In the end, however, Janet gives the client the style she requests just to make her "happy," even though, as a professional, Janet believes it is an inappropriate cut.

The stylists at Pamela's attribute their deference to clients' wishes to a self-sacrificing, nearly maternal attachment. Others researching the hair salon have reported similar findings; for example, Michelle Eayrs has argued that beauticians see themselves not only as helping individual clients (both emotionally and with their appearance) but as benefiting society more generally.[17] At Pamela's, the beauticians say that they often deny their own wishes in favor of their customers' requests; they make these

sacrifices not because of their financial dependence or lower social status but because they care for their clients. For example,
Nancy reports that she focuses on her customers' satisfaction because she is emotionally obliged to do so. She says, "I really do
want to give them what they want [as opposed to what she wants]
because I like all of them and I want to see them satisfied. I'm really concerned...that they're happy with themselves." For this
reason, she gives her clients the haircuts they request even if she
does not like the style. Similarly, Pamela explains her approach
to customers who complain or become overly demanding. She
says, "You just keep your heart open. You try to convey to them,
'I'm here to help you. I'm here to do the best I can for you.' They
realize, 'Hey, it's my time to relax.' They just need to feel they're
as important as everybody else." Pamela is explicitly saying that
she contributes an emotional component to her interactions with
customers. She ensures that no customer feels less cared for than
another, much as a mother ensures that none of her children feels
less loved than the others.

Even though few stylists verbalize their monetary reliance on
customers—presumably this dependence undercuts their claims
to friendship—the commercial nature of the institution limits
beauticians' influence, despite the fact that they rank higher in
the beauty culture hierarchy than do their clients. Stylists depend
on their clientele for salary and autonomy, and so they want to at-
tract and satisfy a large, faithful group of followers who will seek
them out when they move from one salon to another. Trish explains, "If you have a following, you can really work anywhere.
Any salon will take you. Otherwise, if you move, you have to
start from the bottom again, making very little money." Hairdressers negotiate salary depending on their experience and the

size of their clientele, with pay either based strictly on commission or calculated as some combination of a predetermined salary and commission. Additionally, hairstylists receive tips on each procedure they perform, typically amounting to 15 to 20 percent of the total service price. Thus, their incomes increase with the number of their customers.

Not surprisingly, hairdressers' financial dependence on customers shapes their willingness to meet clients' emotional needs and submit to their hairstyling requests. For example, Joanna states, "You don't want them sitting in your chair feeling like you're doing what you want. You have to really listen. If you want this hairstyle and I don't think it's going to work on you, you know I'll give it to you if that's what you want."

While Joanna's statement resounds with sentiments of self-sacrifice, it is clearly shaped by the salon's financial underpinnings. Danielle explains, "If there is a real disagreement, and I'm saying, 'There is no way your hair is going to do this,' and she's like, 'But I want it,' then I cut it the best I can in the way she wants." While Danielle may be certain that she has special knowledge about hair, and may very well try to convince her client that she "knows best," she is financially (and emotionally) compelled to give the customer what she wants.

The beauticians attempt to nullify their status inferiority by conceptualizing hairdressing as both a profession and, somewhat less frequently, an art. For example, when stylists discuss their inborn gift for hairstyling, some liken it to innate artistic talent. Mandy comments, "It's like if you want to be an artist, you don't go to artist school to become an artist. You either are or you aren't." Trish, in contrast, argues that hairstylists meet many of the same needs as therapists.[18] She says that she provides "a lot of the listening, the comforting that somebody goes to a counselor for." While Trish herself admits that she is "not a real counselor," she still claims to give her customers "the same kind of stuff" as a therapist and to "make them feel better." In the end, the stylist is unable to maintain a comparison between herself and a therapist. She recognizes that hairstyling and therapy require different degrees of skill and training.

The hairdressers' conceptualization of their job as a profession is supported by the salon environment. As in a doctor's office, clients interact with several individuals—the receptionist who takes note of the appointment time and services to be provided and the assistant who washes and conditions hair—before actually meeting with the hairstylist. The beautician, it would seem, is too important and too busy to attend to the salon's mundane tasks. Stylists virtually never restock towels, shampoos, and conditioners; they sweep up after haircuts only when all assistants are occupied and one of their clients is waiting for service. These activities typically fall into the domain of the salon assistants, apprentice hairstylists who are not permitted to encroach on the beautician's clearly defined role (or her clientele). According to the rules of the salon, apprentices are not qualified to do the stylist's job. Furthermore, beauticians, like doctors, are detached from financial transactions. Fees are paid to the receptionist rather than to the beautician, and tips are accepted only in containers—most commonly coffee mugs—at the stylists' workstations. In contrast, salon assistants receive tips directly from customers.

Despite the careful cultivation of professionalism, the stylists' professional status is often contested by their clients, many of whom believe that they too have access to stylists' realm of knowledge. Anyone who reads a woman's fashion magazine can learn about the latest trends in hairstyling and beauty products much more easily than a surgeon's patient could educate herself in her doctor's area of expertise. Furthermore, while it is illegal for unlicensed individuals to practice medicine, anyone may cut hair. The ready availability of information from the hairdressers' domain, coupled with customers' skepticism about stylists' understanding of middle-class appearance requirements, allows salon clientele to second-guess their recommendations and preferences.

Generally speaking, beauticians are more similar to service workers than to professionals or artists because their jobs depend in large part on their ability to forge emotional ties with their clients. Even though they may have special skills and talents, they are still financially and emotionally required to defer to the client's judgment. They may try to conceptualize themselves as professionals; they do not, however, have the education or income associated with professional positions. Stylists simply do not wield enormous power with their clients, in part because their emotional labor undermines their claims to professionalism and in part because women who procure beauty treatments in salons are nearly always less embedded in beauty culture than are their beauticians.

PAMELA'S CLIENTS

Donna, an attractive and poised thirty-five-year-old accountant with a three-year-old son, has been a client at Pamela's for nearly three years. When her stylist, Joanna, moved to Pamela's from another local salon, Donna followed her. She comes to the salon every four to five weeks. Joanna colors the gray that began to appear after Donna gave birth and cuts her hair to shoulder length, with wispy bangs. The process costs $70 and takes nearly three hours, time Donna refers to as her "only time to relax and be pampered." Each morning, Donna styles her hair for nearly thirty minutes. Because of her numerous responsibilities at home and at work, she regards this task as a burden and would prefer to wear her hair short. She observes, "After I have my next child and am on leave, I'm cutting my hair short. I can't imagine having two kids and still trying to style my hair." At present, Donna still wears her hair shoulder-length because her husband "won't let [her] cut it," even though short hair is "the style for women now." Donna adds, "Shorter hair is more attractive on women who are growing older. . . . A forty- or fifty-year-old woman with long hair . . . seems tacky to me, like she's trying to be something other than a forty- or fifty-year-old. I think hairstyle has to do with being mature, with being feminine in a way that is suitable for the age you are."

Hair, for Pamela's clients, is part of gender enactment; knowing the appropriate way to wear one's hair at a given point in one's life suggests gender enactment limited by the requirements of aging femininity. While long hair is considered suitable for a young woman, wearing anything but midlength or short hair during middle age reveals either a flawed understanding of appearance norms or a failed attempt to display youthfulness. Donna's current haircut, which is popular with Pamela's clientele, expresses many of the characteristics that Donna uses to identify herself. She comments: "It's a sort of conservative accountant look. It's not tacky; it's a classy hairstyle. It looks more like a nice middle-class hairdo, you know than say, a flashy hairdo. It's feminine without being too frilly. [It's] feminine and simple."

Pamela's clients interpret the meanings of hair, assume that these meanings are shared by members of their social group, and use hairstyle to indicate aspects of the self. Hairstyle is shaped by life circumstances, by competing demands and time constraints; it becomes a site of negotiation between claims of the self, the structure of everyday life, and beauty ideology. Hair for Pamela's clients—as for the stylists—is a display of femininity, but beyond that, it is a display of femininity shaped by the demands of marital status, occupation, income, and age. Hairstyle and its meanings are not free-floating, or absolute, but are instead forged from the structures shaping women's lives.

Pamela's customers discuss their efforts to negotiate an "appropriate" appearance, which includes the ways in which hair indicates self and the processes through which life situation shapes hairstyle. Women value hair that coincides with identity. If their hairstyle misidentifies their age, income, occupation, or education, they feel unsettled and self-conscious. Chris, a thirty-six-year-old doctor, became very upset after having her hair styled. She said, "The cut is atrocious. It's not my image; it's not who I am. It's too dramatic for me. I'm very subtle, but I look like a teenybopper. I told her, 'Don't make me look like someone from Long Island.' There's too much flair and too much pomp and too much stuff in those people's hair. And I walked out looking just like that, which I find not sophisticated."

The new hairstyle associates Chris with a group of people from whom she wants to differentiate herself. While Chris says explicitly that she does not want to be considered a Long Islander, it seems likely that she means that she does not want to be associated with the Long Island working class or lower-middle class. Before her most recent haircut, Chris used her subtle, sophisticated hair to indicate, among other things, that she is a middle-class professional woman. Now, her "atrocious" cut makes her look like the occupant of a less desirable social category. Chris describes her emotional response to the haircut and, hence, to her misidentification: "I was embarrassed, enraged. I was a mess. I was upset. I felt violated. I felt like somebody had taken something they had no right to take and they had done it against my will because I had told her not to…[cut] it [so short]."

Chris also considers this new hairstyle to be inappropriate for her age; she explains that she had wanted to have her bangs cut slightly shorter to add some fullness to hair that was becoming dryer and stiffer with time. Although Chris wanted to "maintain a look [she] had when [she] was younger" by "adding some body and movement," the new cut suggests not that Chris is youthful, but instead that she is immature, unsophisticated, and tacky.

Even though Chris feels that her social location—like her hair—was effectively stolen from her, the change in appearance does not alter her self-concept. Instead, Chris attempts to dissociate herself from her hair by explaining to friends and coworkers that she had not requested the style, wearing hats, and styling her hair to minimize the effect of the cut. She describes her attempts to cover the new style by pulling her bangs back in a headband, but complains that the technique itself seems inappropriate for her age group: "Wearing headbands at my age… it feels like something people five or ten years younger than I am would do. I mean, I'm a doctor. My headband falls down. I have to always be adjusting it. I'm always fooling with my hair."

Clearly, one of the primary aims of the hairstyling session is protecting a middle-class, professional identity. The women are aware that particular hairstyles are interpreted by staff, coworkers, and clients as more "serious" than others. They also recognize that women who work in male-dominated occupations are automatically in danger of failing to appear "serious" enough. Pamela's clients take this danger into consideration when choosing their hairstyles. Elizabeth, a thirty-four-year-old accountant, explains, "I wear this hairstyle, I guess, because I think it's attractive, flattering on me, but also because it is simple. I think it makes me look professional to my clients. If I were walking around with some really big hairdo, I think I'd look less professional."

Although Elizabeth uses her hairstyle to forge a professional identity, she does not disregard the importance of attractiveness. Hair, for Elizabeth, is a display of a particular type of female beauty—one that is "simple" and therefore suitable to her professional status. Moreover, hair involves gender enactment that is closely linked to social class. In a similar example, Vicky, a thirty-nine-year-old teacher, relates her choice of a modest hairstyle to her taste in professional clothing. Vicky says that she "wouldn't walk into class in Spandex" or wearing "one of these curled, teased, and sprayed" styles popular "in the mall." In order to seem like a competent worker, rather than like a woman who spends her days shopping instead of working, Vicky manages her appearance through both clothing and hairstyle.

While only a few of Pamela's clients actually refer to their hairstyles as "middle-class," all of the women use their hairstyles to convey status. Hair, therefore, is more than an indicator of social class; it is also a product of class, particularly in that hair points to taste—that is, to status as opposed to income. Although the women seldom explicitly distinguish their hairstyling choices from those made by women of lower social status, they imply such comparisons by using terms like "classy" and "not tacky" to describe their own hair. The women believe that particular styles—typically the less contrived ones—appear "classy," that is, middle-class, while "big," "poofy," or "flashy" hair does not. Importantly, the "natural" hair that these women desire implies a middle-class lifestyle in which resources are available to provide the healthy food and activities that produce "healthy" hair.

Pamela's clients above all want "natural-looking" hair. However, this quality is related not to its being "natural" in any genuine sense but rather to the painstaking construction of "naturalness." Donna says, "I have to have my hair colored frequently because it seems to get bronzy really, really fast, and I hate that. I don't like anything that doesn't look natural." Donna will not let her hair be gray, its real natural color, but neither does she want it to appear artificial. Ironically, maintaining this less "bronzy" color requires more work than a less natural look would.

More than half of the clients at Pamela's have their hair colored—either with "highlights," in which bleach or dye is applied to selected areas of hair, or in a single-process treatment, in which the colorant is applied to the entire head—and virtually all of them say that they do so because they want natural-looking hair. For these women, "natural" can also mean wavy hair rather than straight, or straight rather than wavy. Some lengths—especially shoulder-length or above—are "natural" and "healthy" looking, as is brunette or "soft" blonde hair, but not black, red, or "bronzy" blonde hair. The styles they describe resonate with images of the straighter, fair hair of Anglo-Saxon ethnicities, that is, of the group that historically populates the middle and upper classes. Furthermore, hair that looks natural does not look unmanaged. The most natural-looking of hairstyles are those created in the beauty salon. "Natural" is, more than anything else, an expression of a taste culture that is specific to a particular social location.

Many of the salon's clients claim to wear natural-looking styles because they care less about their appearance than about having time for other activities. For example, Deirdre, a forty-three-year-old nurse, says, "Five minutes and that's it. I don't like to invest a lot of time in my [hair]. There's other things I'd like to do with my life, more pleasant things, more important things." Hair, Deirdre suggests, is less important to her than other interests, such as speed walking, biking, and gourmet cooking. For this reason, she wears a style that requires little time and effort, a style that she describes as part of an effort to do the "healthiest, most natural thing" for her body in general. However, Deirdre comes to the salon once every four weeks and spends $80 and three hours having her hair colored, cut, and blow-dried. Discussing her hairstyle, Deirdre says, "I make it clear that I don't spend time on my hair. That's why I have her cut it like this." Again, by having "more pleasant" things to do than her hair, Deirdre marks herself as a woman whose priorities supersede the requirements of beauty ideology. In so doing, she effectively resists that ideology.

For customers, unlike beauticians, fashion is tied to particular social locations. As stylists attempt to position themselves as professionals with specialized knowledge, they argue that beauty exists in the absolute, beyond any constraints created by life circumstances or social position. In response to these arguments, customers claim that they have special knowledge that hairstylists do not have about the beauty standards of their own social location. For example, Carol, a forty-one-year-old manager, recalls a disagreement in which the hairdresser argued that Carol's cut needed to be shorter to "look like it's supposed to look." Carol disagreed. She explains her response: "I'm thinking, whose standards are you using? Certainly not the people who I work with."

When the stylist refers to the way that Carol's hair is "supposed to look," her concept of aesthetic correctness is not tied to social circumstance but implies an absolute standard. In contrast, Carol's response suggests that aesthetics are not free-floating. A particular haircut is not absolutely "right" but is "appropriate" or "inappropriate" to an individual's lifestyle and social identity. Hair simply means different things for stylists and their customers.

Women balance their understanding of hair and beauty with responsibilities that shape what hair should look like and determine the amount of attention they can pay to their hair. According to these women, life pressures often win out over their desire to wear feminine or attractive hairstyles. Even when clients agree with beauticians about the styles that make them most attractive, they are sometimes unable to commit the time required to produce them. Anne, the twenty-eight-year-old mother of a newborn, tells her hairstylist that the hectic schedule of childcare forces her to keep her hair long so that she can put it back in a ponytail. She says, "Joanna says I look better with my hair short, but I said, 'Not now, I don't have time.'" Once again, the beautician appears to refer to some natural, correct aesthetic for beauty. Unlike Carol, Anne does not necessarily disagree with her hairdresser's assessment. Instead, she simply disregards it. Anne's life situation, rather than her understanding of beauty or fashion, determines her hairstyle.

Other women dismiss their stylists' advice because they believe that the feminine hairstyles the stylists suggest undermine an appearance of professionalism. Barbara, a fifty-three-year-old marriage counselor, explains, "Danielle says that I shouldn't wear my hair pinned up because it isn't fashionable or attractive. I guess she's right but I say, I want to look like a serious, professional person to my clients, so I just keep pinning it up." Seeing competence and stylishness as incompatible attributes, Barbara styles her hair to accommodate a professional identity.

Several clients explain that they might have different hairstyles if they were younger. Like Donna, these women tend to associate longer hair with youth and shorter hair with maturity. Specifically, they consider shorter hair—that is, hair above the shoulders—more appropriate than long hair for women over forty. Dee, a fifty-five-year-old school administrator, says, "I used to have these long tresses, but I was young and had the svelte body and the lovely face. At the age that I am now, I feel that the more appropriate is a short haircut." Long hair is seemingly linked to an overt sexuality appropriate only for young—and perhaps only young and beautiful—women. Shorter hair, as Donna explains, is "feminine in a way that is appropriate for the [middle] age you are." Dee observes: "You reach a certain stage where you can be sexy without the long hair. There are other components to sex appeal. It's not that appearance is unimportant, but you change your ideas about what is sexy. You grow up in that regard and can be sexy in other ways." Long hair locates one's sexual attractiveness in the physical realm, whereas short hair accentuates a woman's nonphysical sexual attractiveness. In addition, short hair seems to indicate that an older woman knows her proper place. Because she cannot compete with the physical sexuality of younger women, she instead modifies her "ideas about what is sexy."

Pamela's clients bring their own understandings of hair and beauty into the salon, along with a set of experiences that both shape these understandings and structure their choices. Life circumstances limit the value associated with hairstyling as well as the time and money that women are willing to commit to it. Indeed, compared to Pamela's stylists, clients appear practically detached from beauty culture. The two groups of women live in seemingly different worlds, sharing neither social class nor common interests. Beauticians try to forge professional identities and validate their embeddedness in beauty culture by pressing their clients with the belief that beauty and hair are of real and primary importance for all women independent of social status. While their approaches occasionally converge (for example, both groups use hair as part of gender enactment), the two perspectives are more divergent than parallel. Clients remain unconvinced that stylists occupy the same social status as they do and assume that the stylists fail to understand their class-based conception of hair. In the end, they do not see beauticians as artists or experts but as service staff and members of the working class.

WHEN THEY MEET:
THE HAIRSTYLING SESSION

During a hairstyling appointment, beauticians and customers try to ensure that their potentially conflicting interests are satisfied. Selling their emotional labor as well as their expertise, stylists imagine themselves as their clients' social equals and attempt to position themselves as professionals. Clients try to balance the demands of beauty ideology with the challenges they face as professional women.

Because they hold greater social status, customers are far more successful than beauticians at using the salon to accommodate their personal interests and professional identities. While the emotion work of stylists may help them to see themselves as their clients' friends, it is actually a requirement of their occupation rather than an indicator of mutual affection. Specifically, the sharing of personal information operates in only one direction, from client to stylist. Beauticians seldom tell their customers about their own lives or personal problems. Pamela explains, "I feel it's their time. They're here to be pampered, and they may not want to hear about me." If Pamela and her client were truly friends, personal information would be passed both ways. Rather than a friendship, the relationship between beautician and customer is fundamentally an exchange of payment and service. The salon is not a location where women come to share their concerns equally, but rather a commercial environment in which the privilege of self-disclosure is reserved for those who can pay for it.

Stylists provide clients not only with emotional attention but also with haircuts that accommodate their identities and life circumstances. Moreover, they do so at the expense of their own claims to expertise and understanding of hair and beauty. It appears, then, that clients can resist, within definite limits, the influence hairstylists wield as representatives of beauty hegemony. Yet while customers may challenge individual representatives of beauty ideology, the more generalized cultural imperative remains intact. Customers do not question the importance of managed appearance, the need to purchase it, or the definition of femininity based on the accomplishment of idealized beauty. These women obviously feel enormous pressure to conform to contemporary conceptualizations of appropriate adornment,

even though those notions may vary according to a woman's social class, occupation, age, and education. All of the customers
spend considerable time and money in the salon. Even though
they may not yield to the influence of the salon staff, they do not
question the necessity of the salon itself.

CONCLUSION

In the hair salon, women come into contact with representatives of
beauty industry and ideology. Hairstylists reinforce the importance
of commercially managed beauty as part of their own efforts to
nullify status differences between themselves and their customers.
Nevertheless, while hairstylists can easily be conceptualized as a
force in the dissemination of beauty hegemony, the beauticians I
observed were really more victims than victimizers. As the "true
believers" in beauty work, they are committed followers of beauty
imperatives. Beauticians, by way of their low social status and unsuccessful claim to professional identity, are more vulnerable than
their clients to the pressures of the "beauty myth." While their
middle-class customers may very well resist the demands of beauty
ideology in favor of the demands of the workplace, stylists' work
simply serves to reinforce—at least among the stylists themselves—the importance of attaining some notion of ideal beauty.
Furthermore, the stylists are priestesses with a disloyal following.
While their novices clearly hold to many of the crucial doctrines of
the faith, they simply do not trust their leaders. Women may follow some of the cultural mandates of beauty ideology, but these
imperatives do not elevate the position of hairstylists.

While some researchers of gender and occupations have argued that the emotion work women perform creates problems

for identity and self-esteem,[19] I have found that the effects of stylists' emotion work are in truth double-edged. By providing for their clients emotionally, beauticians both support and undermine their own identity claims. On the one hand, by becoming their customers' confidantes and advisers, hairdressers at Pamela's were able to imagine themselves as their clients' friends and, by implication, their equals. Seeing themselves as fulfilling the same purpose as therapists, stylists could again find support for their claims to professional status. Yet because the beauticians pictured themselves as their clients' self-sacrificing, devoted friends, they were forced to put their patrons' wishes before their own professional insights. Even when clients asked for hairstyles that the stylists believed to be inappropriate or unfashionable, beauticians claimed that they were emotionally obliged to provide the requested cuts. Paradoxically, then, beauticians' emotion work allows them to see themselves as their clients' social equals but undermines their claims to professional identity.

The data from Pamela's suggest that more is going on in the world of beauty than cultural critics have heretofore imagined. In contrast to writers like Naomi Wolf, who see beauty ideology as a potent force in women's social disempowerment, I argue that for most women, beauty is not an end in itself. That is, beauty ideology is not monolithic in its power to control women's concerns and behaviors, to limit women's goals, crush their self-esteem, or to keep them economically and socially inferior to men. Rather, women's understanding of beauty is driven by an awareness of social location and cultural distinctions. The causal ordering is, in fact, reversed. Women use beauty work to stress social differences; instead of being its own end, beauty is exploited in the service of social class and status. Beauty ideology is itself of little consequence unless it is useful in other areas of social life.

Obviously, the clients I observed varied considerably in the extent to which they resisted their stylists' conceptualization of beauty ideology. Yet, in most cases, these women claimed that their lives were filled with concerns and loyalties that were simply "more important" than beauty ideology. Considerations of social status, occupation, education, motherhood, and age overrule demands of the sphere of beauty; and in most instances, such concerns reveal themselves to be the women's "higher loyalties." Appealing to these loyalties, then, allows clients to resist stylists' recommendations while simultaneously accepting the larger normative system concerning the professional management of femininity.

CHAPTER TWO

Aerobics

Neutralizing the Body
and Renegotiating the Self

Maintaining a positive identity requires that individuals distance themselves from characteristics and acts that violate social standards.[1] For women, who are valued according to their appearances and whose appearances are—by their very femaleness— flawed, the struggle to construct positive conceptions of selfhood is certainly difficult. They may, as I show in chapter 1, resist beauty ideology by claiming that more important responsibilities like work and family override appearance as an indicator of selfhood. During my research in two aerobics classes, I found that women may also use body work to deny personal responsibility for their appearance. In this setting I observed women negotiating acceptable identities in an institution focused on altering the body—not necessarily by changing the body itself but instead by distancing identity from the body and aligning it with the personality characteristics (like willpower and perseverance) that strenuous body work implies.

In this chapter, I show that women use aerobics as an arena for constructing accounts of the body that position it as an "accident" and so discount the individual's responsibility for physical imperfection. Participants use classes as a resource for renegotiating meanings of body and self, even when aerobics provides little actual physical change. Participation in aerobics allows women to construct accounts of their bodies that, first, release notions of selfhood from the physical and, second, provide a lens through which they can negotiate ideals of beauty. Aerobics provides women with alternative conceptions of beauty and the social context to support those ideals.

Feminists since Mary Wollstonecraft have celebrated women's involvement in sports, claiming that athletics provides confidence and empowerment.[2] Indeed, researchers have shown that women who participate in sports are more likely to be tough-minded, self-sufficient, assertive, autonomous, and emotionally stable.[3] While medical and ideological control of women's participation in athletics continues (albeit in milder forms than in the nineteenth or early twentieth centuries) to limit the types of exercise considered appropriate to proper gender enactment, female athletes now participate in many sports once considered exclusively male terrain.[4]

While men tend to engage more actively in demanding, vigorous sports and recreation, gender differences in overall activity level have nearly disappeared in recent years.[5] Nevertheless, one of the most popular forms of athletics today remains almost entirely the preserve of women. Aerobics is a relatively recent phenomenon in the United States.[6] Deriving its name from aerobic dance-exercise, it includes aspects of sport, dance, and exercise—of both work and play. The first televised aerobics class was broadcast in 1969. In the early 1980s, it was estimated that between 22 and 25 million Americans participated in aerobics and that 90 percent of both students and instructors were women.[7]

Based on the prevalence of workout studios, exercise videos, and gyms, one can only assume that at least as many women participate in the activity today.

At the same time that feminists have lauded sports for women, many have criticized fitness activities like aerobics as examples of contemporary "body management" organized around "the production of self-monitoring and self-disciplining docile bodies."[8] Some argue that, unlike sports such as tennis and swimming, exercise programs like aerobics (especially when run as profit-making ventures) actually harm female participants. Jennifer Hargreaves, in particular, distinguishes these activities from other sports, pointing to their emphasis on weight loss and body toning rather than "fitness and enjoyment or competition."[9] Others argue that activities like aerobics make women more self-conscious about real or imaginary flaws in their bodies, contributing to feelings of self-doubt, insecurity, and personal inadequacy. Furthermore, the "docile" body produced by these activities becomes a "sign of submission" to gender oppression and a mark separating women from each other—setting the toned, active woman against the overweight, inactive one.[10]

I approached my research in aerobics with these critiques in mind. I found, however, that women are capable of using aerobics classes to fuel a construction of self that releases identity from the physical, denies individual responsibility for socially constructed bodily "imperfections," and provides new resources for identity formation.

RESEARCH AND METHODS

From 1991 to 1993, I conducted qualitative research in two aerobics classes on Long Island. The first was part of an employee wellness program (available to faculty, graduate students, and staff) at a local university campus. Run on a not-for-profit basis, this program was intended to promote physical fitness among university employees. In addition to the aerobics class, it included swimming lessons, modern dance and ballet classes, fencing, weight training, and canoeing. The aerobics class was conducted at the university gymnasium three days per week at lunchtime and twice a week in the evenings; participants paid three dollars per class. The lunchtime class focused primarily on cardiovascular fitness, whereas the evening class involved only toning exercises (and is, therefore, more accurately referred to as a "toning" than as an "aerobics" class). The same instructor taught all five sessions (in addition to holding a full-time job as the office manager for her husband's landscaping business). Approximately fifteen women attended the class on any given day.

The second class was held at a Long Island location of a national gym franchise. It was open only to members of the gym. Annual membership cost three hundred dollars and provided access to all gym facilities, including weight-training equipment and cardiovascular exercise machines (e.g., stair-climbers, treadmills, and stationary bicycles). The gym offered around thirty classes per week. The one I joined was called "Funk Aerobics" and, as the name implies, involved high-intensity acrobic dance movements set to fast-paced popular music. The class was held in the aerobics studio, a room with floor-to-ceiling mirrors on two sides and a glass wall at the back, which opened onto the weight-training area. Class members faced toward one mirrored wall and away from the window, so weight lifters could view class participants' backsides without being seen themselves, except as reflections in the mirror. Held on Thursday evenings at 7:00 and seemingly the most popular class at the gym, it was well attended and frequently crowded. I quickly learned that I needed to arrive at least ten minutes before the class started to find a spot near the front. Otherwise, I would be forced to stand in the middle or back of the room, which made it difficult for me to observe the rest of the class in the mirror or to keep up with the class by maintaining a close eye on the instructor. Unlike the university program, the gym offered its members well-padded flooring, state-of-the-art stereo equipment, mats for floor exercises, and a professional, full-time aerobics instructor. Wearing a microphone so she could be heard over the music, the instructor both called out and demonstrated the exercises, which became increasingly intense as the class progressed.

During the two and a half years that I conducted fieldwork in aerobics, I attended the university class five times a week and the gym-franchise class once a week. I observed and talked to class members both during and outside the aerobics sessions. I also made sure to spend ten to fifteen minutes before and after class in the locker room interacting with the women. (I let both instructors and participants know that I planned to write about the class as part of a research project.) Additionally, because some university employees attended both classes, I frequently saw them (and socialized with some of them) outside of class. I paid particular attention to the class members' interactions with each other and with the instructor, as well as to their scrutiny of their reflections in the classroom mirrors. I also attempted to engage participants in conversations about their body work and body image.

In addition to participant-observation, I conducted interviews with twenty-four participants. I concentrated on those I considered to be the core members of the groups, judging by the duration and frequency of their class attendance rather than by their physical fitness or ability. Identifying core members proved much easier in the university than the gym-franchise class. Whereas the women in the university group tended to use the class as their primary source of physical exercise, gym members, who were able to attend any number of the classes offered by the franchise each week, had more variable aerobics schedules. Nevertheless, I focused on the members of the class who attended most regularly.

The sample ranged in age from twenty-two to fifty-five years. All of the women in the university class, excluding one faculty member's wife, were employed by the university as administrators, librarians, secretaries, and instructors. Among the gym class members, I spoke to secretaries, university administrators, accountants, housewives, managers, counselors, students, and librarians. Two of the women in the sample were African American, one was Indian, and the others were Western European or European American. While there were some differences in education and income, the women were, on the whole, middle-class. Two of the women in the sample cited episodes of eating disorders, though neither had been formally diagnosed. Two had undergone cosmetic surgery, one having had rhinoplasty and the other a breast reduction procedure.

The two aerobics classes in no way represent a random sampling of all such activities in the United States or even in New York. They do, however, provide examples of an extremely popular form of body work performed by women in both commercial and noncommercial settings. By studying two classes over an extended period, becoming acquainted with participants, and sharing the aerobics experience with my subjects, I was able to capture the class members' understandings of their work in aerobics, their reasons for participating in body-shaping activities, and the subtle and not-so-subtle purposes that aerobics serves in their lives.

BODY WORK AS DENIAL OF RESPONSIBILITY

As Michael Featherstone, Joan Finkelstein, and others have argued, in contemporary culture appearance symbolizes character, particularly for women.[11] Individuals monitor appearance to present particular images to the outside world. Like most women, participants in these classes fail to satisfy the currently popular "idealised images of youth, health, fitness and beauty."[12] In response to their culturally constructed physical imperfection, the class members attend aerobics to shape their bodies, but, even more important, they also use aerobics to negotiate acceptable identities. That is, whether or not they meet ideal standards of beauty, participants are able, through aerobics, to neutralize the moral meanings ascribed to their bodies. Thus aerobics reduces the "embodiment" of identity by illustrating the positive character traits that are elsewhere taken as incompatible with a flawed body. The willpower and determination implicit in participation in aerobics become more salient components of the self, and the imperfect body becomes less problematic.

During my interviews with class members, I asked each of them to discuss her attitudes toward her body and her reasons for trying to change it. As part of their efforts to explain why their bodies fall short of culturally idealized female beauty, and therefore to minimize their deviance from cultural imperatives, the class members construct accounts of their bodies that involve a time when they felt physically perfect. All the women recall a period when they believed their bodies to be acceptable, or at least not so far from cultural ideals as to violate social norms and mark the women themselves as deviant. For some, this period occurred during childhood; for others it occurred later in life. Clarissa, the forty-eight-year-old university class instructor, says, "I have a picture of myself when I was a little girl. I was thin with long dark hair and nice skin. I remember when the picture was taken, thinking that I was really cute. I thought I was beautiful, and I guess I was." Monique, a forty-five-year-old librarian and member of the university class, recalls similar feelings in early adulthood. She says, "When I was younger, oh, I think I was quite lovely. I had long legs and a nice waist and breasts. Men paid a lot of attention to me. I felt good about how I looked." Clearly, Clarissa and Monique believe that at one point their appearances were unproblematic, if not ideal.

The class members' efforts to change their appearances through aerobics suggest that they have somehow fallen from grace. Indeed, many allude to a specific event that damaged their bodies or, at the very least, altered their perceptions of their bodies. This incident interfered with an implicitly normal developmental process that would otherwise have allowed them to maintain a satisfactory body. In this construction, the body takes on the character of an "accident" rather than a simple product of the aging process or the result of some conscious behavior on the woman's part. These accidents took two forms, one affecting the body itself and the other affecting body image.

Several women claim that their bodies changed in ways that they could not control and with which they did not feel comfortable. Katherine, a twenty-four-year-old librarian and member of the university class, says, "Around age nine or ten, I changed schools and I started to be bussed, like five miles away. And literally, I got fat....It happened within a very short period of time because I wasn't getting any exercise." Similarly, Brenda, a forty-four-year-old secretary and member of the gym class, describes the horror she felt when she gained fifteen pounds around age thirty. She now blames the weight gain on "getting married and feeling tied down, controlled." At the time, she began a program of severe dieting and exercise to lose the weight.

Many other class members also claim that their bodies changed because of something in the environment. The fact that they "lost" ideal bodies is not necessarily a result of behavior or character or even associated with the body. The women had not, for example, been fat all their lives and suddenly decided to lose weight; rather, they originally had ideal—or at least unproblematic—bodies but lost them because of some factor beyond their control. In explaining their problematic bodies as accidents, the class members effectively excuse them—admitting that they are norm violations but refusing to take responsibility for their imperfection. Furthermore, the accidental nature of the physical change implies that it may be correctable. The woman can still reasonably expect to regain her "ideal" body.

The second type of transformative experience altered body image rather than the body itself. Several women stated that a heterosexual partner told them that their bodies failed to meet cultural standards of beauty. Colleen, a forty-two-year-old administrator and member of the university aerobics class, says that her efforts to lose weight began as a response to comments from her husband. Soon after their marriage, he made several remarks encouraging her to exercise in order to change her "chubby" body.

Colleen says, "He was like, 'Let's get out there and run.' He made me, I mean, he didn't make me do it, but we went from the doorway to the end of the block, and I thought I would die." Liza, a thirty-four-year-old graduate student who occasionally attends the gym class, remembers that she had always felt physically attractive until a boyfriend pointed out her appearance "flaws." She says, "My boyfriend would take my thigh and squeeze it so you could see the cellulite and say 'Look at this, look at this…it's disgusting,' and I would say 'Have you ever been with a woman who didn't have any of that?' He said 'Yes, I have.'"

Other women developed a sense of their physical imperfection from family members. Most report that males in their households were not similarly pressured to conform to notions of idealized masculinity. Terry, a thirty-two-year-old accountant and member of the gym class, recalls that her younger brother was never encouraged to diet or exercise. She says, "[His weight] wasn't an issue; it was a female thing." And Sandra, a twenty-five-year-old student who attends the university class, remembers that, even though her brothers and father frequently criticized her appearance—with comments like, "You wear a [size] large! Just how much bigger are you planning to get?"—they never pointed out each other's physical flaws.

These incidents, too, take on the character of accidents in the class members' accounts. That is, each woman's body image deteriorated because of the negative comment of a significant other. The blame for their negative perceptions of self lies with the individuals who criticized their bodies, not with the women themselves or even with their actual appearances. Many class members claim that they now realize that such negative comments were unfounded. For example, Monica, a fifty-five-year-old medical technician and member of the gym class, tells me that criticism from her mother concerning her appearance during her teens made her believe that she was overweight and unattractive. Despite the negative feelings these criticisms provoked, Monica says that she now realizes that she was not an unattractive young woman. She states, "I look at pictures of myself when I was that girl my mother made feel so horrible. I was short, yes, but not more than a couple pounds overweight. I had a lovely smile and a nice face, pretty eyes, and good hair. I really had no reason to feel so bad, but I did...because she told me I needed to lose weight, that I needed to 'do something' with myself." Monica implies that without her mother's negative comments, she could very well have maintained a positive body image. Her feelings of inadequacy derive from her mother's criticisms, not from any real flaws. Her negative body image is, in essence, an accident caused by the comments of another.

As Featherstone argues, the body does indicate selfhood,[13] but the link between self and body can be renegotiated through work on the body, such as aerobics. This process is evident in the accounts women generate about their bodies and the relationship between body and identity. Participating in athletics implies a set of positive personality attributes—including strength, perseverance, and stamina—that reduce the importance of the body for selfhood. The body may continue to be flawed, but participation in aerobics neutralizes its relation to identity.

Women use aerobics to set goals for themselves, such as "making it through the entire class," "attending every class for two weeks," and "doing all three sets of sit-ups." Achieving these goals, in turn, allows the women to see themselves more positively. For example, Katherine suggests that her ability to complete the aerobics class makes her feel like a successful, capable person. She says, "I feel good because I've never been one of the 'best' people [in a class]." Notably, Katherine's participation in aerobics provides positive consequences for self, despite the fact that her body has visibly changed little since she began attending the class. She says, "I can do most of the [exercises]...even if I'm not the thinnest." Similarly, Lydia, a thirty-three-year-old day-care worker and member of the gym class, explains, "I guess my body hasn't changed a lot since I started [doing aerobics], but the way I feel about myself has. At least now I know I'm the kind of person who cares enough about herself to do something good for herself." Participating in aerobics has clear identity implications; the activity becomes evidence that the class members are determined, that they are valuable and, hence, worth caring for, that they, like Katherine, are good enough or even "the best." Their aerobics activity tells a different story about these women than do their bodies, which remain imperfect.

Each class member attempts to construct an identity that does not rely on the flawed body, negotiating the relationship between self and body while attending aerobics classes and often undertaking additional activities such as jogging, weight lifting, and walking. The importance of physical activity becomes especially obvious when the women cannot attend aerobics classes because of an injury or a busy schedule. During these times, the women are less able to forgive themselves their imperfect bodies. The body is no longer neutralized and, in the absence of an alternative indicator of character, impinges more heavily on self-esteem. For example, MaryAnn, a thirty-three-year-old teacher who attends aerobics at the gym, says that after missing classes for three or four days, she begins to feel undisciplined and out of shape because, as she puts it, "Somehow not exercising makes me much more neurotic about what I'm eating." When she cannot take aerobics, she focuses greater attention on her body. Other class members describe feeling "really panicky"; they perceive their bodies as "fat and flabby" and say that they are unwilling to weigh themselves. After missing a week of classes, Michelle, a thirty-three-year-old graduate student and member of the university class, says, "My pants are fitting, but now they're getting tight, and I'm like, 'Oh shit. This is no good.' Like I was leaning over…see how tight they're getting. I get these indentations in my skin." Attending aerobics regularly, on the other hand, makes the class members feel "virtuous," "physically better, maybe because of the endorphins," and "like giving myself a break."

Many of the women also participate in other activities to alter their appearances, including following a diet and paying attention to makeup and clothing. Nevertheless, in a paradox similar to that of aerobics, the energy they expend in these areas allows the women to claim identities based on determination and self-discipline rather than on appearance alone. Outside aerobics, food restriction is the predominant way the women shape appearance and attempt to neutralize the body's effect on self-image. For example, Michelle observes, "I eat the same stuff all the time. Every morning I have a buttered bagel. If I deviate, I'm really uncomfortable. Like if I have eggs on it I have to take away half the roll and just eat that half with the egg. So there's ways I can adjust it, but I've got to be real careful." By placing strict limits on food consumption, Michelle is able to feel comfortable with her body and thus less focused on it for her identity.

Similarly, Regina, a forty-three-year-old administrator in the university class, says that she eats sporadically to control her weight and never eats in the evening, even though she cooks dinner for her family. Her strict eating regime causes her to eat while sleepwalking. Nevertheless, she claims that her diet is essential for controlling her perceptions of self. As she herself acknowledges, she is probably not eating less by skipping dinner and eating in her sleep. She told me that she usually consumes four to five hundred calories every night. She would not, she claims, eat while sleepwalking if she ate more during the day. Yet strict control of her daytime food intake is important in that it suggests that Regina has discipline and self-control. Presumably, she does not hold herself responsible for eating while she sleeps.

The positive personality implications of aerobics, as well as the other strategies that the women employ to control appearance, help them accept bodies that will never be perfect. Furthermore, the women's renegotiation of the significance of the body for selfhood reduces the influence of prevailing notions of feminine beauty. For example, Eleanor, a thirty-three year-old consultant in the gym class, says that she has come to accept that she will never look like "the women in swimsuits," and while she admits that "that's not a nice feeling," her work in aerobics has helped reduce the power of the body to signify self. She accepts her appearance because she can "look reasonably attractive, as long as I have all my clothes on," but she now focuses on being a healthy, active person who refuses to "let myself get too crazy worrying about my body."

MaryAnn says that she has reconciled herself to being heavier than women she describes as "long, lanky model beauties." She claims to worry little about her weight because participation in aerobics has allowed her to focus instead on her body's physical capabilities "and even changing my ideal of how I think I should look." These women do not have to mold themselves to contemporary notions of ideal feminine beauty because, for them, the body is diminished as an indicator of self. Failing to meet popular notions of beauty is no longer a failure of character. Within certain recognizable limits, a flawed body is only a flawed body.

Nevertheless, many of the women still describe some degree of connection between the imperfect body and individual identity. Most waver between positive and negative attitudes about their appearances and the character flaws those appearances imply. Clearly, there are limits to women's ability to maintain positive feelings about body and self in the face of cultural and social messages to the contrary. For example, Carmine, a twenty-five-year-old student in the gym class, says that while she recognizes that the currently glamorized female appearance is "just a socially constructed image of beauty and that the ideal is not a natural one," she simultaneously "buy[s] into all that ideology and think[s], 'Oh, I need to do better.'"

Carmine's statement exemplifies many of the women's perceptions and interpretations of their bodies. Some deal with this dilemma by occasionally allowing themselves lapses in self-discipline, particularly in eating. Eleanor explains that her current strategy for dealing with body image is premised on "not getting sucked back into being too obsessed. So, for instance, if I get really upset now, I might sit down and have two or three peanut-butter-and-jelly sandwiches." In this instance, Eleanor actively and self-consciously opts not to allow herself to invest identity in her body. She rejects the cultural association of body and self and chooses to prohibit herself from becoming "obsessed" with glorified images of female beauty.

The women use several methods for neutralizing the body's effect on self-image. While each method is related to body image and appearance, each has implications that extend beyond the body. The class members use aerobics and the other forms of body work described here in two ways: first, to create a sense of control over their bodies, and, second, to reduce the stigma of a flawed body by demonstrating that it is not indicative of a flawed character. As a result, they are able to emphasize the personality implications of body work, rather than the imperfect body, as they construct selfhood.

BODY WORK AS CULTURAL RESOURCE

Aerobics not only supplies a foundation for negotiating female identity; it also serves as a cultural resource for alternative conceptualizations of female beauty and provides a social context to support these alternative ideals.[14] Aerobics acts as one of many possible vehicles for "femininity," "female beauty," "fitness," and "attractiveness." Importantly, it not only makes these images available to the women who participate in it but also serves as an arena in which women can rework these ideals.

Many class members have adopted notions of female beauty that they see as challenging idealized femininity. These ideals overwhelmingly take the form of a toned, muscular physique, albeit within the range of acceptably feminine muscularity. While numerous feminist writers have discussed this body form as no more liberating than the glamorized image of women as physically thin and frail,[15] or as simply the current stylish body type for women, others have seen the potential for this body type

to stand as a symbol of "empowerment and escape from traditional images of femininity and domesticity."[16] The class members themselves discuss their muscular female ideal as counter-
ideological and personally liberating. While a muscular female
shape requires an enormous amount of physical effort to acquire
and maintain, and as such can be criticized as absorbing energy
that might be better spent in other activities, it provides a goal
that involves strength rather than weakness, activity rather than
passivity, and a personal choice about one's appearance rather
than acceptance of culturally glorified images. Overall, the
women's discussions of their aerobics participation testify to the
fact that any given culture produces numerous, often conflicting,
values and ideals. Moreover, these values and ideals exist within
and are supported by distinct social contexts.

The concept of woman as athlete flourishes in the context of
aerobics classes and provides a physical goal that participants find
satisfying and personally empowering. During aerobics, the
women push themselves to run faster, kick higher, and jump far-
ther with each class session. In the gym-franchise class, the women
were able to watch themselves in the mirror, and I often observed
them challenging themselves with stern, fixed stares. All the
women showed an intense interest in their body's ability to accomplish physical challenges, and many reveled in their physical
power. The women yelled, stomped their feet on the wooden
floors, clapped their hands, and sang along with the music. They
became wrapped up in the physical experience of the aerobics
classes. In this sense, aerobics gives women the opportunity to re-
joice in their strong, muscular bodies and physical power, rather
than producing the "self-disciplining docile" bodies criticized by at
least one feminist theorist.[17] By rejecting the cultural ideal, which

they describe in terms such as "tall," "long-legged," "impeccably emaciated," "extremely thin, probably unhealthily thin," and "bones everywhere," the women excuse their own bodies' deviations from it. They imply that they would not take on this glamorized feminine form even if they could, and so they undermine its value and effectively neutralize their violation of current beauty standards.

In an explanation of the body to which she aspires, Beth, a twenty-five-year-old student in the university class, says that her physical ideal has changed since she started aerobics. While she once hoped to become "very thin," she now has a "more muscular ideal," characterized by "strength, ability, stamina." She says that she realizes that she will never be "model" thin and that longing for an extremely svelte figure is self-destructive. She claims that by idealizing a muscular female body, she has "a better chance of getting where I want to be." Samantha, the twenty-eight-year-old instructor of the gym class, says that she often feels pressure to have a "perfect body, especially since I teach aerobics." Samantha suggests that she knows that she will never have a body "like a model," and so has "decided that it is really better to be fit, toned, muscular." This muscular ideal of female beauty, in turn, allows her to "feel in pretty good shape...pretty attractive, pretty proud." The women idealize a body type that is compatible with the work they do in aerobics. For all the class members, a muscular, well-proportioned physique is considerably closer to their own bodies and to the bodies they may achieve through their body work than is the very tall, skinny, air-brushed image glorified in beauty pageants, magazines, and recent movies.

Some feminists have argued that the physical effort expended in aerobics creates bodies that symbolize submission to male oppression.[18] They argue that the toned, taut body—which is rarely achieved by any but the most ardent of aerobics participants, and then only by those with the proper genetic predisposition—is a sign of internalized domination and self-regulation. Furthermore, several observers have claimed that the popularized physical end product of aerobics has less to do with activity or physical capability than with a superficial "look."[19] However, in adopting their own idealized female body type, the women in the aerobics classes focus on both the physical capabilities of this physique and the identity to which it attests. Rather than seeking only to appear fit, the women are explicitly aspiring to a body that can complete physically demanding tasks. They work toward bodies that appear both athletic and sexual and can perform athletically and sexually. Emily, a thirty-five-year-old bookkeeper and member of the university class, says that she likes having a body capable of physically challenging activities. She says that it is important to her to "have the tone and the definition when I move that people can see that I use [my body] and am strong and sexual...[my ideal of beauty] is about being able to do what I want with my body." And Carmine explains that even though she has never before felt capable or strong, aerobics makes her confident that she "can do things physically." Carmine sees the increase in her muscularity as evidence of her physical ability. She says that her new perspective on the importance of physical capability has allowed her "not to worry about being thin," but instead to "focus on muscle tone." Her physical goals now relate more to strength and ability than to bodily reduction.

Many of these women idealize not only a specific body type but also the personality that their ideal body type implies. While the physique that these women idealize involves a certain appearance and a set of abilities, it also involves competence and self-confidence. Olivia, a fifty-three-year-old manager who attends the gym class, explains that being in shape helps her to feel more powerful in everything she does. She says, "If I look strong and feel strong, people will sense that when they meet me. I'll be more effective." And MaryAnn notes that for her, attractiveness "is even more an issue of confidence than an issue of appearance." Aerobics, she says, helps build that confidence.

If this muscular female ideal is simply one more example of male domination, as has been argued by some feminist writers, it is nevertheless one that these athletes select because it provides a more positive foundation for selfhood. While I never observed these women discussing alternative images of beauty, they frequently talked about the changes that aerobics has made in their bodies and the changes they hope to make. In fact, the women create a shared idealized body by designing, within the structure of the aerobics class, the bodies to which they aspire. Aerobics provides an arena where women can not only work on achieving their idealized body type but can also find social support from other women for an image of beauty that, to some extent, undermines current norms for femininity.

One of the many feminist criticisms of fitness activities like aerobics is that these enterprises become, at least in their popularized depictions, "settings for female narcissism and competition rather than for companionship and co-operation."[20] While this criticism implies that members of aerobics classes feel rivalry, aerobics has also been criticized for producing a body type that separates women who exercise from those who do not.[21] However, the participants interviewed for this research attest to the importance of connections built with other women in aerobics.

Instead of competition, these women espouse feelings of camaraderie with other class members. For example, Jeannette, a
twenty-five-year-old student who attends the gym-franchise
class, says, "It's fun to see the same faces every week....Sometimes during really tough parts of the routine, one of the other
women and I will look at each other and kind of roll our eyes.
It's like, 'Don't worry, we'll make it.'" Jeanette garners support
and companionship, as opposed to competition, from her classmates. At the same time, there are limits to this companionship,
created in part by the class structure and in part by the competing demands of class members' lives. The loud music and intensity of the exercise prohibit long conversations, and while some
members (particularly of the university class) converse before and
after aerobics, others arrive at the last minute and rush out after
class to get home or back to work.

Notably, several of the members of the lunchtime aerobics class
attend with friends. The women suggest that the class serves a
special purpose in their relationship. For example, Wanda, a
forty-three-year-old secretary, claims that attending the university class with her friend has become one of the ways they provide
support for each other. She says, "When one of us feels down, the
other will make sure she gets to aerobics. It's a kind of deal we
have." In contrast, most of the participants of the gym-franchise
class were not friends before they began attending aerobics. Generally, these women focus on the shared experience of class participation. Lucy, a thirty-year-old emergency medical service
provider, says that even though she often comes to the class feeling sad or tired, the other women's enthusiasm and their "yelling
and laughing" cause her to get "caught up in their fun" and lift
her spirits. Likening the gym aerobics class to "a modern-day

quilting bee," Sarah, a thirty-three-year-old counselor, claims that going to aerobics is in part motivated by a desire to share time with her acquaintances in the class.

Additionally, when the class members compare their own bodies to those of women who do not exercise, they tend to highlight the positive feelings they gain from their efforts. Rather than experiencing separation from women who do not participate in aerobics, they instead gain self-confidence from compliments that these other women give them. Jessie, a forty-five-year-old secretary, says that her female coworkers tell her that she has "a young-looking body." Even though Jessie notes that her body "isn't perfect by any means," she takes enormous pleasure in these compliments. Importantly, she does not respond by feeling superior to or distant from the women who make them but instead invites them to attend aerobics with her. Few of these women focus on the putatively narcissistic or competitive aspects of these activities. Instead, even beyond finding support for alternative conceptions of female beauty, they use aerobics to build or deepen female relationships, share accomplishments, and take pleasure in compliments received from women outside the class.

CONCLUSION

Aerobics becomes a method for neutralizing the flawed body and a resource for constructing an alternative physical ideal. Rather than a source of self-doubt, domination, and disruption, aerobics is a method for modern women to work out issues of considerable significance. Living in a society that conceives of women's bodies—and of women themselves—as flawed requires women to renegotiate cultural images to construct nondeviant identities.

Women in contemporary Western society encounter ideals of womanhood and women's bodies that are impossible to attain, at least in part because they are internally contradictory. In activities like aerobics, women attempt to negotiate identity with regard to cultural ideals of femininity, resisting those ideals on certain levels, accepting them on others, and creating alternative ideals when they are useful.

Contemporary society's emphasis on the body makes it a location where much of selfhood is grounded. This emphasis makes it difficult for individuals to dissociate identity from corporeal experience and physical appearance, even when that appearance is flawed. Efforts to transform the body become efforts to transform identity and to alter the relationship between body and self. Aerobics allows participants to see themselves as possessing character traits that, once incorporated into the self, can negate the implications of a stigmatized body. Additionally, aerobics serves as one of many cultural resources for counter-ideological notions of the feminine while providing female social support for those ideals.

Some feminist writers have criticized aerobics, claiming that activities organized around shaping the female body, almost by definition, support a system of male domination. Nevertheless, aerobics provides women with a cultural resource that helps them negotiate issues related to beauty ideology, femininity, and gendered identity. I have shown that aerobics participants do not passively accept cultural constructions of idealized femininity but instead put such activities to use as they position themselves individually in relation to the ideology of beauty.

CHAPTER THREE

Cosmetic Surgery
Paying for Your Beauty

After several unsuccessful attempts to schedule an appointment, I finally managed to meet with Jennifer, a twenty-nine-year-old grade school teacher who volunteered to talk with me about her cosmetic surgery. On a typically cold November afternoon, I spoke with Jennifer in her apartment on the south shore of Long Island. Jennifer is 5 feet 6 inches tall and has long, straight blonde hair and expressive light blue eyes. That day she was dressed in an oversized gray pullover and black sweatpants. While we talked, she peeled and sliced the crudités that would be her contribution to the potluck engagement party that she was attending later that evening.

During our conversation, I noticed that by far the most prominent feature in her small studio apartment was the enormous black and chrome stair-climbing machine set slightly off from the center of the living room/bedroom. I learned that Jennifer spends forty minutes each day on this machine and works out with weights at a nearby gym three to four times a week. She eats no meat, very little oil or fat, and no sweets, and she drinks very little alcohol. Despite her rigorous body work routine, Jennifer's legs have remained a disappointment to her. Rather than lean and muscular, they look, by her account, thick and shapeless— particularly around her lower thighs and knees. Jennifer says that her decision to have liposuction was motivated primarily by her inability to reshape her legs through diet and exercise. During the procedure, the fatty deposits were removed from the insides of Jennifer's knees, making her legs appear slimmer and more toned.

Jennifer acknowledged her own significant ambivalence about taking surgical steps to alter her body. If possible, she would have preferred to shape her legs through aerobics, weight training, and dieting, rather than through liposuction, which Jennifer described as a final and desperate option. By her account, plastic surgery was the only way to alter physical attributes that she referred to as "genetic flaws," features that she could change through no other available means. Expressing some shame, as she says, "for taking the easy way out," Jennifer's guilt is not so great that she regrets having surgery. Indeed, she plans to have a second liposuction in the near future, this time to remove the fatty tissue from her upper and inner thighs.

Cosmetic surgery stands, for many theorists and social critics, as the ultimate invasion of the human body for the sake of physical beauty. It epitomizes the astounding lengths to which contemporary women will go to obtain bodies that meet current ideals of attractiveness. As such, plastic surgery is perceived by many to be qualitatively different from aerobics, hairstyling, or even dieting. In this view, cosmetic surgery is not about controlling one's own body but is instead an activity so extreme, so invasive that it can only be interpreted as subjugation. Even more than women who may participate in other types of body-shaping activities, those who undergo cosmetic surgery appear to many observers—both casual and academic—to be so obsessed with physical appearance that they are willing to risk their very existence to become more attractive.

Not surprisingly, cosmetic surgery has been attacked by the scores of feminist writers who criticize body work generally.[1] While these attacks may be well deserved, the cosmetic surgery industry is expanding rapidly nevertheless. Board-certified plastic surgeons performed more than 2.2 million procedures in 1999, a 44 percent increase since 1996 and a striking 153 percent increase since 1992. Liposuction, the most common cosmetic procedure in the United States, was performed 230,865 times (up 57 percent since 1996 and 264 percent since 1992), at a cost of approximately $2,000 per patient. Breast augmentation, with its price tag of nearly $3,000, was the second most common procedure, at 167,318 (a 51 percent increase since 1996). Blepharoplasty (eyelid surgery), the third most common, was performed on 142,033 patients at a cost of just under $3,000, followed by face-lift (72,793) at over $5,000, and chemical peel (51,589), at nearly $1,300.[2] Ninety percent of these operations are performed on women, as are virtually all breast augmentations and reductions, 87 percent of liposuctions, 91 percent of face-lifts, and 85 percent of blepharoplasties. In 1999, American women had 167,318 breast augmentations, 120,160 blepharoplasties, 201,083 liposuction procedures, and 66,096 face-lifts.[3]

Although strategies for surgically altering the body's appearance have been available for centuries, the practice has only recently become a mass phenomenon. Until recently, patients were most often men disabled by war or industrial accidents. Now the recipients are overwhelmingly women who are dissatisfied with their looks.[4] Today, aesthetic operations make up 45 percent of all plastic surgery.[5]

Cosmetic surgery is one of the fastest-growing specialties in American medicine.[6] Although the total number of physicians in the United States has little more than doubled in the last quarter of a century, the number of plastic surgeons has increased fourfold. At the end of World War II, there were only about 100 plastic surgeons in the country; in 1965, there were 1,133. By 1990, that number had tripled to 3,850. Moreover, these figures may underrepresent the total number of individuals performing aesthetic procedures today. Because it is not necessary to be a licensed plastic surgeon to perform cosmetic surgery, procedures such as face-lifts, eyelid corrections, and chemical peels may be performed by other specialists, such as dermatologists.[7]

Criticisms of surgical alteration of the female body multiply nearly as rapidly as the procedures themselves. One of the main critiques of cosmetic surgery derives from the dangers involved. Cosmetic surgery is undeniably painful and risky, and each operation involves specific potential complications. For instance, pain, numbness, bruising, discoloration, and depigmentation frequently follow a liposuction, often lingering up to six months after the operation. Face-lifts can damage nerves, leaving the patient's face permanently numb. More serious complications include fat embolisms, blood clots, fluid depletion, and even death. Health experts estimate that the chance of serious side effects from breast augmentation are between 30 percent and 50 percent. The least dramatic and most common of these include decreased sensitivity in the nipples, painful swelling or congestion of the breasts, and hardening of the breasts that makes it difficult to lie down comfortably or to raise the arms without shifting the implants.[8] More serious is the problem of encapsulation, in which the body reacts to foreign materials by forming a capsule of fibrous tissue around the implants. This covering can sometimes be broken down manually by the surgeon, but, even when successful, the procedure is extremely painful. When it is unsuccessful, the implants must be removed; in some cases, the surgeon must chisel the hardened substance from the patient's chest wall.

Clearly, the recipient of cosmetic surgery may emerge from the operation in worse shape than when she went in. Unsuccessful breast augmentations are often disfiguring, leaving the patient with unsightly scars and deformation. An overly tight facelift produces a "zombie" look, in which the countenance seems devoid of expression. Following liposuction, the skin can develop a corrugated, uneven texture.

Finally, some criticisms of plastic surgery focus on the implications of such procedures for contemporary conceptualizations of the body and identity. Cosmetic surgery has expanded alongside specific technological developments, including advances in medical equipment like magnifying lenses, air drills for severing bone and leveling skin, and improved suturing materials, all of which enable surgical interventions to be performed with better results and less trauma for the patient.[9] According to some critics, these developments, and the increasing flexibility in body altering that they permit, are linked to cultural discourses likening the body to what Susan Bordo has called "cultural plastic." The body is now understood as having a potential for limitless change, "undetermined by history, social location or even individual biography."[10] Not only has the body come to stand as a primary symbol of identity, but it is a symbol with an unlimited capacity for alteration and modification. The body is not a dysfunctional object requiring medical intervention but a commodity, not unlike "a car, a refrigerator, a house, which can be continuously upgraded and modified in accordance with new interests and greater resources."[11] The body is a symbol of selfhood, but its relation to its inhabitant is shaped primarily by the individual's capacity for material consumption.

Of the various forms of body work, plastic surgery is surely the hardest to justify. The physical dangers are real. The symbolic damage done to all women by the apparent surrender of some to unattainable ideals of beauty is significant. Yet the criticisms also leave out a good deal. Most important, the criticisms operate either at the grand level of cultural discourse or the highly grounded level of physiological effect. As a result, they overlook the experience of the women who have plastic surgery. In this chapter, after first discussing the role of the doctor as a gatekeeper to plastic surgery, I focus on that experience.

First—and most important to those who undergo it—plastic surgery often works. This fact stands in contrast to a rhetoric that concentrates on the unattainable character of contemporary beauty ideals, portraying plastic surgery as a Sisyphean task. Critics of plastic surgery imply that those who undergo it will complete one operation only to discover some new flaw. Yet this is not the case. Somewhat to my surprise, many of the women I interviewed expressed enormous satisfaction with their procedures.

While some did, indeed, intend to return for additional operations, others seemed content to have fixed a particular "flaw." I
do not mean to argue that all contemporary ideals of beauty are,
in fact, attainable. They are not. Neither do I mean to argue that
women in contemporary America can escape the nagging self-
doubts caused by those unattainable ideals. They cannot. But the
ambitions of those women who undergo plastic surgery often
stop far short of attaining ideal beauty. And given these limited
ambitions—and within the cultural space marked out for the expression of female beauty—plastic surgery frequently achieves
the exact goals intended by those who undergo it.

Second, criticisms of plastic surgery directed at gender issues
often understate the extent to which this activity involves gender
at an intersection with age, race, ethnicity, and even class. Many
women surely undertake plastic surgery, most notably in the case
of breast enlargement, to enhance distinctively female attributes.
Others, however—Jewish and Italian women who have rhinoplasty, Chinese and Japanese women who have their eyes reshaped—do so in a distinctively ethnic context. And many others have plastic surgery in an attempt to reproduce the bodies of
their youth. If plastic surgery speaks to the depredations of gender domination, we should recognize that it also speaks to the
depredations of Anglo Saxon ideals of beauty and the idealization of youth.

Third, the criticisms of plastic surgery ignore the complicated
process by which the women who undergo surgical procedures
integrate them into their identities. If not in feminist theory, then
in popular culture, there lies an implicit notion that the benefits
of plastic surgery are somehow inauthentic and, therefore, un-
deserved. Although the critics of plastic surgery insist that ap-

pearance should not be the measure of a woman's worth, the women who have plastic surgery are nonetheless participants in a culture in which appearance is taken as an expression of an inner state. To be able to purchase a new nose or wider eyes or thinner thighs seems then to sever the relationship between inner states and their outer expression. Where the women in aerobics classes are working hard to detach their identities from their bodies, the women who undergo plastic surgery must work even harder to reattach their identities to their new appearances. On the one hand, they are using plastic surgery to tell a story about themselves: I am the woman with svelte thighs or a button nose. On the other hand, they must also tell a story about plastic surgery in order to counter the charges of its inauthenticity. They must somehow show, to themselves even more than to others, that the new appearance is both deserved and a better indicator of the self than the old appearance—an appearance necessarily repositioned as "accidental." The result, then, is that the woman who has plastic surgery finds herself in a double bind. She is unhappy with her appearance, and so she takes the only steps she can to improve it. No matter how successful her efforts are—or how pleased she is with their outcome—the woman must ultimately defend her decision to purchase appearance and identity.

RESEARCH AND METHODS

The research for this chapter involved fieldwork in a Long Island plastic surgery clinic and interviews with the surgeon and twenty of his female patients. Finding a location to study cosmetic surgery proved difficult because many women hesitate to admit that they have undergone such procedures and physicians are bound by doctor-patient confidentiality. Having organized my research around interviews and fieldwork in identifiable physical locations, I knew that I wanted to talk with a single surgeon's female patients, rather than a "snowball" sample of surgery clients, whom I could have located easily through advertisements in local newspapers, gyms, universities, or hairstyling salons. As a result, I needed to find a cosmetic surgeon who would permit me access to patients. My search for this doctor took nearly six months, during which time I contacted over twenty clinics and interviewed seven physicians.

I eventually chose to focus on the clinic of Dr. John Norris, a local surgeon specializing in aesthetic procedures. My discussions with the six other physicians proved to be a rich source of data about the cosmetic surgery industry and cosmetic surgeons themselves. I learned, for example, that cosmetic surgeons are frequently critical of their female clientele, seeing them as obsessed and impossible to please. Moreover, often believing that the physical imperfections that their clients observe are insignificant, surgeons sometimes suspect their patients of trying to solve emotional problems by altering their bodies.

I met John Norris at the gym where I studied aerobics. As a member of the gym, I spent a considerable amount of time there each week, both in research and on my own body work. John and his wife, Monica, were gym regulars who, like me, tended to exercise in the mornings, and I saw them several times each week. Even though I had met him previously, I contacted John formally, as I did the other cosmetic surgeons in the area. I explained my project to his receptionist and made an appointment to speak with him. After our second meeting, I asked John to allow me to interview twenty of his female clients. He agreed and asked his receptionist to contact women who might be willing to talk with me. After obtaining his patients' approval, John provided me with their names and telephone numbers. This procedure surely biased my sample in favor of successful cases. In addition to interviewing patients (one of whom I was able to interview both before and after she had surgery), I conducted several interviews with John. I also attended informational sessions at another local clinic to learn more about many of these procedures.

John conducts his enormously successful practice in two offices, one on Long Island and the other in Manhattan. I spoke with him at some length about his interest in aesthetic plastic surgery. He explained that although he had originally aspired to be a sculptor, he soon decided that a career in art would not provide an adequate income. As his interest in science developed, John opted instead for a medical career and for what he now refers to as the "excitement of sculpting human appearance." Believing that his work helps his patients to feel more satisfied with the way they look, more desirable, and more confident in their professional and private lives, John says that he derives enormous satisfaction from his career.

John is interested not only in "sculpting" the appearances of others; he is himself heavily involved in the culture of body work. In particular, John has participated in bodybuilding since he was fifteen years old and, at age fifty-one, still participates regularly in bodybuilding competitions. Moreover, John has personally undergone plastic surgery to remove the "love handles" that he says will develop at his waistline unless he maintains a body composition of no more than 3 percent body fat. As his medical career has progressed, John's training and competition have both fueled and been fueled by his interest in using surgery to rework the aesthetics of the body. While he began his career doing recon-structive and burn-correcting surgery in addition to cosmetic procedures, he now focuses almost exclusively on aesthetic plastic surgery, which he finds equally rewarding and more enjoyable.

Similar to the staff of Pamela's Hair Salon, John is a "true be-liever" in beauty ideology. Like the stylists, John not only dispenses the means of altering appearance but also is deeply involved in reworking his own appearance. Nevertheless, he is differentiated from them by his higher social status. Like Pamela's staff, John is able both to assess his clients' appearance "flaws" and to suggest particular techniques for correcting them. But, unlike Pamela's staff—and primarily because of his status as a medical profes-sional—John's patients nearly always accept his advice. Simply put, John is different from Pamela's stylists because he not only dispenses "beauty" to his patients but also shapes the choices they make about their appearances.

Moreover, John regularly denies surgical candidates access to the body work he provides. He is selective in choosing his clien-tele, screening patients to ensure that they are suitable for the op-erations they request. Listening to the client's description of her physical imperfections, John determines whether or not her com-plaint is reasonable—whether or not her nose is really inappro-priate for her face, her breasts are really too small, her ankles are really too thick, and so on. In making such judgments, John (like the beauticians at Pamela's) blurs the line between technique and aesthetics, effectively broadening his area of expertise. While un-derstanding his activity as a process of determining the "appro-priateness" of surgical candidates, he actually selects patients based in large part on his personal taste and sense of aesthetics.

As a purveyor of body work, John positions himself not only as a surgeon but also as an expert in contemporary standards for female beauty.

In deciding whether patients are suitable candidates for the procedures they request, John judges not only the aesthetics of their appearance but also their psychological health. By his own account, John attempts to determine whether patients are trying to deal with personal crises (such as divorce) through plastic surgery. John says that when he talks with potential patients about their motivations for having cosmetic surgery, many express sadness or fear regarding a significant personal relationship, even to the point of breaking down in tears in his office. This reaction, he claims, suggests that patients should seek the services of "some other type" of professional—presumably, a psychologist or marital counselor—rather than those of a cosmetic surgeon.

John has come to categorize patients in four conceptual types, distinguished primarily by their motivations for having surgery. The first of the groups includes individuals who are "self-motivated and realistic." These patients pursue surgery as a means of bringing their appearances in line with their inner self. Claiming that their bodies fail to represent them as the people they truly are, individuals in this group explain their desire for cosmetic surgery with statements such as "I don't feel like an old person. I don't want to look like one," or "I exercise and diet. I want to look like I do." These candidates, according to John, are adequately prepared for cosmetic surgery, with expectations that will likely be met by the procedures they undergo.

The second type of patient seeks out plastic surgery to please someone else. In John's description, this patient—usually a woman—is going through a painful breakup and, hoping that changing her appearance will reignite her partner's interest, turns to plastic surgery as a "last-ditch effort" to save her relationship. Breast augmentation—which, John notes with some amusement, is the surgical procedure most likely to precede divorce—is a common request among members of this category. John typically refuses to perform such procedures on patients who hope to use plastic surgery to solve some personal problem.

The third group in John's typology involves children, usually brought to the office by their parents. According to John, these patients' parents frequently say things such as "She has her father's nose," which the parents, rather than the children themselves, judge as unattractive and requiring change. John makes it a practice to ask the adolescents what they think about the particular body part. According to him, they tend to be relatively satisfied with the "nose" or other problematic feature, finding it far less objectionable than the parents do. John advises parents not to "fix what isn't broken," to give the child a few years to "grow into" the feature and then broach the topic of surgery again if they feel it necessary.

The last group includes individuals John refers to as "flighty," who want surgery for any number of "bizarre" reasons. As an example, John described one woman who wanted to have rhinoplasty because a favorite movie star had undergone the procedure. In another case, a potential patient requested breast augmentation in order to look more like a celebrity her boyfriend admired. In such cases, John refuses to operate because he considers these individuals to be psychologically unstable and impossible to satisfy.

All told, John claims that he rejects two or three requests per week. His ability and willingness to deny service suggest another comparison between the plastic surgeon and the hairstylist: John is less dependent on his clientele than are the beauticians at Pamela's, who have little choice concerning whose hair they style or how they style it. At the same time, John's decisions to reject patients are linked to his medical and legal responsibility for the surgeries that he performs. Indeed, his motivations for denying surgical procedures suggest a wariness about trying to satisfy the desires of individuals whose expectations are unreasonable and who might hold him legally responsible for their inevitable dissatisfaction. In this sense, John is even more vulnerable to his clients than are the stylists at Pamela's. While a beautician might lose a client who dislikes her haircut, John could potentially lose much more to a patient who claims that he is responsible for some physical deformity, particularly if that patient decides to sue.

The patients I interviewed ranged in age from twenty-four to fifty. The procedures they underwent included breast augmentations, nose jobs, face-lifts, eye-reshaping procedures, tummy tucks, and liposuctions. All of the women were Asian American or European American; three were of Semitic ancestry; and all but one (a full-time mother) held salaried jobs or were students at the time of the interviews. They were employed as opticians, medical technicians, receptionists, insurance agents, teachers, office administrators, hairstylists, and secretaries.

THE STORY OF A FACE-LIFT: ANN MARIE

Ann Marie, a slender, soft-spoken fifty-year-old medical technician with upswept blonde hair, was one of the first patients I interviewed. Married to her current and only husband for nearly thirty years, Ann Marie carries herself with a careful gentility.

Dressed in snug-fitting woolen pants, low-heeled brown pumps and a fuzzy light mauve sweater, Ann Marie invites me into her small, tidy home and asks if I would like coffee. Anxious to begin my first interview, I refuse. Ann Marie brings her own drink back from the kitchen in a tiny, flower-painted china cup and saucer and begins telling me about her experiences with plastic surgery.

Ann Marie is not at all shy about discussing her face-lift. She actually seems eager to tell me the reasons for her decision. Her appearance began to change in her late thirties and forties when she developed "puffiness underneath the eyes" and "drooping upper eyelids." Most unattractive, by Ann Marie's account, "the skin of my throat started getting creepy." In her words, "You get to an age" when "you look in the mirror and see lines that were not there before." Because her physical appearance had begun to reflect the aging process, she explains, "All of a sudden, the need [for cosmetic surgery] was there."

While Ann Marie describes her need for a face-lift as "sudden," she had planned to have the procedure long before. She recalls that "about ten years ago," she spoke with several close friends about having a face-lift at some point in the future. She explains, "We talked about it a long time ago. I guess I have never accepted the axiom of growing old gracefully. I have always sworn I would never picture myself as a chubby old lady." Ann Marie and her friends "talked and decided that when the time was just right, we would definitely do it." Ann Marie is the only member of the group who actually went through with surgery.

Despite her resolve, Ann Marie did not enter into cosmetic surgery lightly. Instead, for several years she "thought about it from time to time. There was a lot to be considered." Among the issues she contemplated were the physical dangers involved in the operation, the risk of looking worse after the surgery than before, and the importance of choosing a well-qualified doctor with an excellent reputation. She explains, "You are putting your face in the hands of a surgeon; there is the possibility of absolute disaster, very possibly permanently. You have to choose the surgeon very carefully."

Ann Marie chose John Norris to perform the face-lift. Largely because he had performed an emergency procedure for her just over one year earlier, Ann Marie claims that she felt completely comfortable with him. "John was recommended to me by my dermatologist. I had an infection on my face; it was quite serious. The dermatologist told me I had to go to a plastic surgeon, and John was the only one he would recommend." Because of the dermatologist's recommendation and her satisfaction with John's earlier work, Ann Marie returned to him for the face-lift. She visited his office in Long Island for a consultation and, not long after her appointment, decided to go ahead with the procedure.

During their first meeting, Ann Marie had what she refers to as two "surprises": one was the price of the operation and the other the news that she would have to stop smoking. According to Ann Marie, John explained that "you will not heal as well if you continue to smoke. Because it impedes circulation, smoking decreases your ability to heal properly." She says, "The most difficult part was to stop smoking. I was puffing away a pack and a half a day for over twenty years." John told Ann Marie that she would not be able to smoke for three months before the surgery. She says, "I thought, What? I will never be able to do this. But I did, I stopped cold. That was the real sacrifice for me."

While giving up cigarettes may have been the greatest sacrifice for Ann Marie, there were clearly many others. For a full year, Ann Marie had to work "one day job, one night job, occasionally a third job" to afford the surgery. She had to "bank" four weeks of overtime at her primary job so she could take time off to recover from the procedure. She also postponed repairs on her home. She explains, "There were things my house needed, but my feeling was, I needed a face-lift more than my house did."

By providing me with a long and detailed account of her need for a face-lift and the sacrifices she was willing to make to have the procedure, Ann Marie hints at an awareness that her behavior is somehow subject to criticism, that it might be construed by others as superficial or shallow. With a hint of defensiveness, Ann Marie explains that she "needed" the face-lift—despite its financial costs and physical risks—not merely because she is concerned with her appearance, but because of pressures in "the workfield." She says, "Despite the fact that we have laws against age discrimination, employers do find ways of getting around it. I know women my age who do not get jobs or are relieved of jobs because of age.... [The face-lift] will ensure my work ability." Ann Marie, by her account, decided to have cosmetic surgery not due to narcissism but to concern for her professional well-being. Justifying her behavior as a career decision, she implies that she is sensitive to the social disapproval of plastic surgery, that she knows that the behavior requires some justification.

Even though Ann Marie believes that looking younger will help her professionally, she also admits that she has "not seen anything that has really changed in that area." Instead, the procedure has affected her primarily "on a personal basis, a social basis." Explaining these effects in more detail, she says, "I meet people I haven't seen for two or three years who will say, 'There is something different about you, but I don't know what it is.' I met a sister of a very good friend of mine in June, which is five months after my surgery. She looked at me and said, 'I don't know you.' I said, 'Of course you do. I've known you nearly all of my life.' She realized who I was and was astounded at my appearance."

This incident, along with several similar ones, has, by Ann Marie's account, improved her self-image. By attributing these experiences—and the resulting improvement in her self-perception—to her face-lift, Ann Marie justifies her decision to have cosmetic surgery. In contemporary Western culture, "feeling good" about oneself is understood to be worth considerable effort because it makes us better workers, spouses, and citizens. Among children, self-esteem is credited with the ability to improve grades and to discourage sex and illegal drug use. Ann Marie explains her choice to have plastic surgery as "a matter of personal esteem. If you feel you look better, you feel better about yourself." By granting cosmetic surgery the power to provide self-esteem, Ann Marie—like many of the other women I spoke with—effectively legitimizes an otherwise illegitimate activity.

At the same time, Ann Marie's defensiveness suggests that she is somewhat self-conscious about her choice. She describes her decision to have a face-lift as "not purely vanity," and then adds, "If it is vanity, so what? That does not make me a bad person. I don't want to look bad. I don't want to look my age. I want to look younger. I want smoother skin." By her account, Ann Marie is not "bad" or vain; in fact, she is actually a good person, as evidenced by the other forms of body work in which she participates. She explains, "My weight is only a variance of six pounds heavier from what it was thirty years ago. I keep in shape in addition to the surgery. I jog, I exercise, I diet." Ann Marie has maintained her physical appearance of youth in every way possible—failing only to control the appearance of her facial skin, which she could not keep from "getting creepy." In her account, Ann Marie deserved the surgery—an act tinged with deception—because she has proved her moral character through other (physically demanding and highly symbolic) forms of work on her body. Ann Marie is entitled to an appearance that reflects those efforts, even if that appearance is obtainable only through cosmetic surgery.

"A DEEP, DARK SECRET": HAVING LIPOSUCTION

John arranged for me to speak with a twenty-seven-year-old woman named Bonnie who was planning to have cosmetic surgery. In sharp contrast to the other women I interviewed, Bonnie was hesitant to speak with me about the procedure, because, as she later said, she considered it to be "a deep, dark secret" that she had discussed with no one but her husband of five months. Bonnie worked out at the same gym that both John and I attended. Because she and I were previously acquainted, John suggested that Bonnie speak with me about the procedure she was considering, and she agreed. Over the next six months, Bonnie and I met several times to discuss cosmetic surgery; during that period, she decided to have liposuction, underwent the procedure, and recovered from it.

Having recently completed a master's degree at a New England university, Bonnie moved to the east end of Long Island to take a position as a chemist in a pharmaceutical firm. She explained to me that over the years she had spoken casually to various women about cosmetic surgery and had "fantasized about" having liposuction herself, though she had never considered it seriously. Prior to having the operation, Bonnie told me why she was reluctant to have cosmetic surgery:

> It's always seemed to me to be one step too far. I have dieted and exercised my whole life, and sometimes I've gone over the edge and done some things that probably weren't very healthy, but I could always stop myself before I became totally obsessed. I guess I have always thought that I would never get so obsessed that I would allow my body to be cut into just so I could look better. At least that's what I had always hoped. I couldn't imagine myself as one of "them," as one of those weak women who would go that far.

Despite her stated objections to cosmetic surgery and her characterization of its patients as "weak," Bonnie underwent liposuction on the outside of her upper thighs. Bonnie described this area of her body as "flabby, no matter what I do. I exercise five or six times a week; I cycle with my husband. I do all the weight lifting that is supposed to tone up the muscles in those areas. Nothing works!" Nevertheless, Bonnie never seriously investigated the procedure until she finished graduate school and began full-time employment. She explained, "This is the first time I've ever made enough money to think about doing something like this. The liposuction will cost $2,000, which is less than it usually costs because I won't have to have general anesthesia, but it's still a lot of money."

Referring to her new job and home, Bonnie noted that she would never have considered having cosmetic surgery while she was living near her family and friends. "I wouldn't want any of my friends or my family to know about it, only my husband. My family would all be like, 'You don't need to have that done. You're crazy. You are thin enough already.' That doesn't keep me from thinking these lumps on my thighs are really ugly. They are the only thing I see when I look in the mirror."

Bonnie's hesitance to discuss liposuction with her friends stems from her perception of cosmetic surgery as part of a process of "giving in to pressure, giving in to these ideals about how women should look, when none of us real women are ever going to look like that." Bonnie believes that her friends would react to her interest in plastic surgery by making her "feel so ashamed, like I am not strong enough to accept myself like I am."

Unlike most of John's patients, Bonnie articulates her ambivalence about plastic surgery primarily in political rather than personal terms. Her description of her friends' imagined objections is one of many examples of her concern with the political meaning of her actions. In another, Bonnie explains that her own political view of cosmetic surgery is the main source of her conflict over having the procedure. She says, "I am not worried about problems with the operation itself. I know that Dr. Norris has a great reputation. I've talked to other people at the gym who have used him, and they were all really happy. He does so much of this stuff, I'm sure he's really good at it." Bonnie's concerns focus instead on the social and cultural significance of her action. "If I am proud to be a woman, then I should be proud to look like a woman, with a woman's butt and a woman's thighs." Reacting to her own accusations, she notes, "I am proud to be a woman, but I really hate it when I get a glimpse of my backside and I just look big. I feel terrible knowing that it is those areas of my body which are understood to be most 'female' that I dislike the most." Expressing her interest in cosmetic surgery as her only viable option for reducing her dissatisfaction with her appearance, she adds,

> I don't really know how to get around it, though, because I really do not like those parts of my figure. Plastic surgery seems like a pretty good way, and really, a pretty easy way, to deal with that dissatisfaction, to put those negative feelings behind me ... to move on with the rest of my life.... I'd love to get dressed for work in the morning and have only the work in front of me, rather than, you know, what's literally behind me, be the thing that concerns me the most.

Bonnie is explicitly aware that the body and the self are linked. When she says that she dislikes the "female" parts of her figure, one can easily imagine replacing the term "figure" with the term "self." Indeed, it is Bonnie's ambivalence about her female identity that is most troubling to her; eradicating the physical signs of femininity—and the flaws inherent in those attributes—may enable her to construct a self that she believes to be less imperfect, more culturally acceptable, and that will allow her to focus more attention on other activities and concerns, including her career, the sports she enjoys, and her new marriage. At the same time, her decision to undergo liposuction comes at a considerable cost; Bonnie says explicitly that, if possible, she would prefer to change her perceptions rather than her body. The "pressure" she feels, however, limits her ability to rework her self-image, leaving her to choose between plastic surgery and a negative self-concept, two options that are unsatisfying. Bonnie's decision to undergo liposuction suggests that, in the end, the costs associated with plastic surgery are somehow less significant than those attached to her appearance flaws.

Obviously, Ann Marie and Bonnie present two quite disparate facets of the concerns women face as they consider having cosmetic surgery. While Ann Marie struggled to meet the financial and physical requirements of her face-lift, Bonnie agonized over the political dimension of her decision to have liposuction. So distinct are these preoccupations, in fact, that they can be conceptualized as opposite ends of a continuum, along which the perspectives of the other eighteen women I interviewed can be placed. For most of these women, the political implications of cosmetic surgery, though not entirely insignificant, were far less important than they were for Bonnie. The other women I interviewed were more often concerned with the health risks and financial costs of cosmetic surgery and with how they would look after their procedures.

While Ann Marie's and Bonnie's preoperative anxieties took different forms, both constructed elaborate justifications for plastic surgery. Like the other women I interviewed, Bonnie responds to the negative identity implications of plastic surgery by explaining that she has done all that is humanly possible to alter an imperfect body but that no act short of plastic surgery will allow her to live peacefully with herself. Invariably, the women's accounts involve bodies that were flawed in some way for which the individual claimed not to be responsible. Each woman's body was imperfect not because she had erred in her body work but because of aging, genetics, or some other physical condition that she could not control. Their flawed bodies are inaccurate indicators of character, and so they effectively lie about who the women really are. Accounts like these permit women to engage in cosmetic procedures with less guilt. Plastic surgery becomes for them not an act of deception but an attempt to align body with self.

"THE BODY I WAS MEANT TO HAVE": WHY WOMEN HAVE COSMETIC SURGERY

Whereas some writers have dealt with cosmetic surgery as if it were an attempt to attain idealized female beauty in order to gain the approval of men,[12] the women I interviewed claim that their goal in undergoing plastic surgery is neither to become beautiful nor to be beautiful specifically for husbands, boyfriends, or other significant individuals. Rather, they alter their bodies for their own satisfaction, in effect utilizing such procedures to create what they consider a normal appearance, one that reflects a normal self. While I do not accept their accounts without some skepticism, I believe that women who have plastic surgery are not necessarily doing so in order to become beautiful or to please particular individuals. Instead they are responding to highly restrictive notions of normality and the "normal" self, notions that neither apply to the population at large (in fact, quite the reverse) nor leave space for ethnic variation. Plastic surgery "works" for women who have these procedures, but it works only within the context of a culture of appearance that is less about beauty than it is about control based on the physical representations of gender, age, and ethnicity.

My respondents claim that prior to having surgery, some particular physical feature stood in the way of their looking "normal." This feature distinguished them from others and prohibited them from experiencing "a happy, regular life," as Marcy, a twenty-five-year-old student, put it. Marcy decided at twenty-one to have the bony arch in the middle of her nose removed and its tip shortened. Before the procedure, Marcy had never been involved in a romantic relationship, a fact that she attributed to her "hook" nose and unattractive appearance. Marcy says, "I have always felt terrible about how pronounced it was. No matter how I wore my hair, it was in the middle of my face, and everybody noticed it. It's not like I could just wear my bangs long."

Marcy decided to have rhinoplasty near a date that was particularly symbolic for her. "I was having my nose done just before Valentine's Day. I thought to myself, maybe if I have my nose done for Valentine's Day, by next Valentine's Day, I'll have a Valentine!" Although she did not find a Valentine for the following year—she explained that dating "didn't happen until a few years later"—Marcy claimed that over time, the surgery allowed her to experience pleasure that she would otherwise have missed.

Because Marcy uses cosmetic surgery to make herself more appealing to others, her experience seemingly supports the criticisms of authors like Naomi Wolf. However, Marcy stresses that she does not expect plastic surgery to make her beautiful. Neither does she believe that winning male affection requires her to be beautiful. Quite the contrary, Marcy clearly imagines that a merely normal appearance is sufficient to garner the male attention she desires.

The women describe several ways in which their physical features have kept them from living ordinary lives. For example, Barbara, a twenty-nine-year-old bookkeeper, says that her breasts—which were, by her account, too small to fill out attractive clothing—made her appear "dumpy" and ill-proportioned. Her "flaw" contributed to a negative self-image, which in turn served to limit the education and career goals Barbara set for herself, the friendships she fostered, and the romantic and sexual relationships she pursued. Barbara decided to have her breasts augmented (from a 36A to a 36D) to become, in her words, "more attractive to myself and others." While her larger breasts have in fact made Barbara feel more attractive, she, like other patients I interviewed, nevertheless laments women's inability to be self-confident despite their physical shortcomings. She says, "For women, the appearance is the important thing. That's too bad that we can't worry about not being judged. [Small breasts] made a big difference in how I felt myself being perceived and how I felt about myself as a person."

Because physical attractiveness shapes the way women are "judged," appearance must be protected as women age. Like Ann Marie, several of the patients I interviewed underwent cosmetic procedures aimed at reducing the natural signs of aging. These women claim that aging had changed an acceptable appearance into an unacceptable one that reflected negatively on their identity. For instance, Sue, a forty-four-year-old optician, decided to have the loose skin around her eyes tightened. She discusses her motivations for having the operation: "My eyes had always been all right, nice eyes. I guess I had always liked my face pretty well, but with age, the skin around them started getting puffy. They just didn't look nice anymore. I looked tired, tired and old. That's why I had them fixed." While Sue had, according to her own account, once been satisfied with her appearance, she grew to dislike her face as the signs of aging became apparent. She used cosmetic surgery to regain the face she liked "pretty well."

Several women told me that they chose to have cosmetic surgery not to make themselves beautiful or outstanding in any particular way but simply to regain normal physical characteristics they had lost through aging.[13] Like Sue and Ann Marie, Tina, a forty-eight-year-old receptionist, used cosmetic surgery to combat the physical changes associated with growing older. Tina underwent liposuction to reduce what she referred to as "secretarial spread," the widening of her hips and buttocks that she believed had come with her twenty-five-year career in office management. She explains, "When I was younger, I had nice hips, curvy but narrow enough, and my rear was well-shaped. After a lifetime of sitting, growing older and flabbier, it had gotten really huge." Tina hoped to restore her appearance to its more youthful form. Believing that her only means of doing so was cosmetic surgery, Tina opted to have liposuction rather than surrender to the aging process that had so drastically altered her body.

Youth—or at least a youthful appearance—is not the only characteristic women attempt to construct or regain through aesthetic procedures. Indeed, three of the patients I interviewed—all under the age of thirty—had cosmetic surgery to reduce the physical markers of ethnicity. These women underwent procedures intended to make their physical features more Anglo-Saxon. Marcy, a Jewish woman, notes that her rhinoplasty removed physical features "more frequently associated with Jewish people." Jodie, a twenty-eight-year-old student who also had her nose reshaped, says, "I had this Italian bump on my nose. It required a little shaving. Now, it looks better." By a "better" nose, Jodie implies a more Anglo-Saxon, less Italian, and therefore less ethnic nose. And Kim, a twenty-two-year-old Taiwanese American student, underwent a procedure to make her eyes appear more oval in shape. She said, "[Taiwanese people] regard girls with wide, bright eyes as beautiful. My eyes used to look a little bit as if I was staring at somebody. The look is not soft; it is a very stiff look." While none of these women consciously attempted to detach themselves from ethnicity, they nevertheless chose to ignore the fact that their efforts to appear "normal" explicitly diminished the physical markers of that ethnicity. Seemingly indifferent to this loss, they accept the notion that normalized (i.e., Anglo-Saxon) features are more attractive than ethnic ones.

All the women claimed that plastic surgery was, for them, a logical, carefully thought-out response to distressing circumstances that could not be otherwise remedied. They now perceive themselves to be more socially acceptable, more normal, and, in several cases, more outgoing. As Bonnie explains, "I got exactly what I wanted from this. My body isn't extraordinarily different, but now, I feel like, well, I have a cute bottom. I have a cuter figure. I don't feel like the one with the big butt anymore. And for me, that lets me put my body issues away pretty much."

At the same time, displaying some remnants of her original ambivalence about cosmetic surgery, Bonnie notes, "I wish that I could have said, 'To hell with it, I am going to love my body the way it is'…but I had tried to do that for fifteen years, and it didn't work." She adds, "Now, I know I'll never look like Cindy Crawford, but I can walk around and feel like everything is good enough."

Women who undergo plastic surgery report various other benefits. For instance, some say that they can now wear clothes that they could not have worn prior to their operations; others attest to having greater self-confidence or to being more extroverted. Jennifer explains, "When I walk out that door in the morning, my head might be a little bit higher when I'm wearing a certain outfit. Like, before I had [liposuction] done, it used to be, I feel good, but I hope no one will notice that my legs aren't too nice."

These women now wear bathing suits, dresses with low-cut necklines, and feminine and revealing lingerie. Wearing these clothes, and believing themselves to be attractive in them, shapes the women's perceptions of themselves and increases their self-confidence. Tara, a twenty-seven-year-old student, told me that before she had breast augmentation surgery, she avoided wearing bathing suits in public and rarely shopped for bras. She says, "[Breast augmentation] has given me more self-confidence than I ever had. I fit in when I'm with my girlfriends now. Before, I never went to the beach with anybody around. After I had [plastic surgery], I couldn't wait to buy a bra. I could never buy one before because I was so pathetically small." Having plastic surgery made Tara appear more "normal." She is now able to participate in activities from which she previously felt excluded.

Barbara, who also had breast augmentation surgery, recounted a similar experience. She says, "I used to wear super-padded bras when I dressed up, but they just never did it for me. I didn't look like the other women. But now, like tonight, I am going to a party, and I know I'll be able to fill out the dress." She added, "[Breast augmentation] has made me feel very confident. I think that's the difference."

Sandra, a forty-three-year-old office manager who had liposuction to reduce her "thick thighs" and "saddlebag" hips, explains that she underwent the procedure not only to appear youthful and wear feminine clothing, but also to approximate a cultural ideal involving social class. "I used to put on nice clothes and still look like a bag lady, you know, unsophisticated. Now I feel like I can wear good clothes and look like they are appropriate for me. Now, my body fits the clothes." Sandra likens appearance to a tableau of social class, both in the context of the clothing one chooses and the extent to which one's body appears to be "appropriate" for that clothing (and the social standing that it implies). Simply put, before Sandra's surgery, her "flabby" body had less class than her clothing. Her body undermined her efforts to use appearance to stake out a particular social location. In effect, it not only made her clothing an ineffective class identifier but also invalidated her claims to a particular status. Plastic surgery, however, has allowed Sandra to display social class through clothing. Cosmetic surgery legitimizes Sandra's claims to social status.

Other women I interviewed also claimed that cosmetic surgery helped them feel more self-confident. For example, Kim says, "I guess I feel better when I am out with friends, like maybe people will think I am attractive. I feel attractive and I guess, I act more attractive." Thus, the women imagine that they are now perceived more favorably and so behave in a manner that they believe is appropriate for "attractive" women. At the same time, the women recognize that they may simply be imagining others' perceptions of them and that their behaviors may have changed independent of any alteration in the way they are viewed. Kim says, "Maybe nobody even notices, but I feel like I look better. I guess just thinking I look better changes the way I act a little."

Nearly all of the women told me that their romantic partners believed the cosmetic procedures were unnecessary. Before her breast augmentation procedure, Tara's boyfriend voiced significant apprehension. "He was very, very frightened about it. He kept on telling me, 'I love you just the way you are,' that type of thing." And Barbara's fiancé blamed himself for her dissatisfaction with her breasts. She recalls, "My fiancé thought he was doing something wrong that would make me feel like this about myself." In many cases, the women's partners attempted to convince them not to undergo the surgery. Jennifer says her boyfriend "tried to talk me out of it, but finally he decided, 'If it's going to make you happy, go

ahead and do it.'" Some of John's patients report that their partners have had mixed reactions to the results of the procedures. Barbara says that even though she has always considered her husband
a "breast man, because his eyes would pop out if he saw a big-
breasted woman," he nevertheless told her that she was "perfect"
with small breasts. She adds, laughing, "He still says he liked me
better before, but I'll tell you, I can't keep him off of me. I keep saying I'm taking them back for a refund."

The frequency with which I heard such assertions points to the
considerable importance women attach to having "freely" chosen
to have cosmetic surgery, independent of coercion by their lovers
or the desire to please someone other than themselves. These assertions make sense in light of the women's accounts of their surgery. Plastic surgery cannot be both something women "deserve"
and something that they are forced or manipulated into doing. In
their accounts, plastic surgery is positioned as a final option for
correcting a tormenting problem. This conception of plastic surgery is clearly inconsistent with an image of acts forced on them
by others—particularly others who might actually benefit more
from the procedures than do the women themselves.

PLASTIC SURGERY AND INAUTHENTICITY:
THE HIGH PRICE OF BODY WORK

In turning "abnormal" bodies into "normal" ones, plastic surgery
succeeds: the woman who participates in plastic surgery comes
to possess the foundation (i.e., a normal body) of a normative self.
However, plastic surgery fails as a method for constructing a positive self-concept because of the negative social and political
meanings attached to it. Women participate in cosmetic surgery

in a world that limits their choices and in which the flawed body is taken as a sign of a flawed character. Despite the negative connotations of plastic surgery, women opt to engage in such procedures because the alternative is more detrimental to self-image. However, most of the women I interviewed carry with them the burden of their decisions; the process of dealing with that burden exacts from them a considerable price.

Some of the costs of cosmetic surgery—including the danger of physical damage and the high financial price—are obvious to those who have undergone these procedures and perhaps even to those who have not. Most of these women had plastic surgery only after serious consideration (often accompanied by research into the medical technology involved in the operations). Likewise, few could easily afford the surgery they underwent; nearly all of them had to sacrifice some other large purchase or to weather financial hardship. Some have accrued considerable debt, while others had to request financial help from relatives. Only a very few of the women had health insurance that covered part of the cost.

Other costs associated with cosmetic surgery, while less concrete, are no less substantial. Specifically, after surgery, women must attempt to deal with the taint of inauthenticity these procedures imply. Although the body appears more normal, the character becomes suspect, with the self, by implication, becoming deviant. The unacceptable act of cosmetic surgery displaces the normative body as an indicator of character. Although the women I interviewed do not formulate the complexities and contradictions involved in their activities in the way I have here, their accounts show that they struggle with a self-concept that continues to be deviant despite their now-normal appearance. Indeed, the accounts themselves—which attempt to deny inauthenticity by positioning cosmetic surgery as somehow owed to the women who partake of it—show that plastic surgery fails to align body and self.

These accounts suggest a singular conclusion with regard to the success of plastic surgery for establishing the normative identity. Women like Ann Marie and Bonnie—like participants in the aerobics classes—invoke their rigorous body work regimens as evidence of moral rectitude and as the basis for their entitlement to cosmetic surgery. But although cosmetic surgery patients and aerobics participants seem to rely on the same symbols of identity, for women who undergo cosmetic surgery, those symbols fail to mitigate the body's negative implications for self. Had these women accepted their body work as an adequate indicator of identity, they would not have needed to turn to plastic surgery to correct their bodies' failings. Moreover, still needing to establish the "deceptive" act of plastic surgery as irrelevant to self (and to position the surgically altered, normative body as the true indicator of selfhood), these women revert to accounts that have already proved unsuccessful. Indeed, the negative implications for self inherent in cosmetic surgery require women to resort to accounts that they know—consciously or not—fail to support the normative identity. In so doing, these women attest to the failure of cosmetic surgery to position the transformed body as symbolic of self. Simply put, if plastic surgery were a successful method for constructing identity, these women would argue that the surgically altered body—rather than body work that has proved unsuccessful at shaping the body or establishing the self—serves to symbolize identity.

CONCLUSION

My research points to three general conclusions. The first bears on the reasons women have plastic surgery and suggests a modification of the criticisms of such procedures. The second bears on the ways in which women create accounts of plastic surgery, which are ignored by the criticisms of plastic surgery to date. The third returns more sympathetically to those criticisms.

None of the women I spoke to embarked casually on plastic surgery. The costs associated with these procedures—measured in dollars and the risk of physical damage—are well known. Although physicians may serve as gatekeepers by preventing some women from undergoing surgery, they rarely recruit patients directly. When surgeons actively market their practices—as did John Norris—they tend to do so indirectly, through advertisements in local magazines and shopping malls. And the women I interviewed did not report that they underwent surgery at the urging of a husband, parent, lover, or friend. Rather, the decision to seek surgery seems to have been theirs alone, at least in the immediate circumstances. To be sure, these decisions were shaped by broader cultural considerations—by notions of what constitutes beauty, by distinctively ethnic notions of beauty, and, most important, by the assumption that a woman's worth is measured by her appearance. Yet to portray the women I talked to as cultural dupes, as passively submitting to the demands of beauty, is to misrepresent them badly. A more appropriate image, I would suggest, is to present them as savvy cultural negotiators, attempting to make out as best they can within a culture that limits their options. Those who undergo plastic surgery may (ultimately) be misguided, but they are not foolish. They know what they are doing. Their goals are realistic, and they in fact achieve most of what they set out to accomplish with plastic surgery. Although their actions surely do, in the long run, contribute to the reproduction of a beauty culture that carries heavy costs for them and for all women, in the short run they have succeeded in their own limited purposes.

Second, plastic surgery requires a defense. Much like the women I studied in the aerobics classes, those who underwent plastic surgery are working hard to justify themselves. But the accounts of the women who have plastic surgery are very different from those of the women who attend the aerobics classes. The aerobics women use hard physical work as an indicator of character that allows them to sever their conception of the self from the body. In contrast, the women who have had plastic surgery work hard to reattach the self to the body. First, they must convince themselves that they deserve the surgery, whether by the hard work they put in at the gym or the effort they invest in saving the money for the procedure. In so doing, they make the surgery psychologically and ideologically their own. Second, they must convince themselves that their revised appearance is authentically connected to the self.[14] To do this, they invoke essentialist notions of the self and corresponding notions of the body as accidental, somehow inessential or a degeneration from a younger body that better represented who they truly are.

I do not mean these observations as a defense of plastic surgery so much as an effort to understand that surgery and its implications. Indeed, if we are to distinguish plastic surgery from other forms of body work, we can do so on precisely the grounds I have just suggested. I am not convinced that reducing facial wrinkles is somehow less "real" than dyeing hair from gray to brown or even that eye surgery or rhinoplasty is somehow less authentic than a decision to have straight rather than curly hair. However, what characterizes the efforts of women in aerobics, hair salons, and, as we shall see, in NAAFA, is that they attempt, in somewhat different ways and with varying degrees of success, to neutralize appearance as a measure of character. Far more than the other women I studied, the women who undergo plastic surgery help to reproduce some of the worst aspects of the beauty culture, not so much through the act of the surgery itself as through their ideological efforts to restore appearance as an indicator of character.

My own criticisms of plastic surgery are tempered by observations of the women described in the other chapters of this book. Although I have characterized plastic surgery as a research "site," parallel to an aerobics class or a group of women in a hair salon or the members of NAAFA, this parallel is in certain respects misleading. In the hair salon, in the aerobics class, and especially in NAAFA, I found women working together to find common solutions to a shared problem. But the women who underwent plastic surgery were not a group in the same sense. For the most part, they did not know each other. They did not speak to each other. And although they may have had common problems with a common solution, they did not develop this solution cooperatively. In the other settings I studied, the local production of an alternative culture was very much in evidence. In the plastic surgery group, however, there were the aesthetic judgments of the plastic surgeon, the ignored opposition of friends and family, but no culture of its own. The women in the aero-

bics class, in the hair salon, and especially in NAAFA, all chal-
lenged a beauty culture, however haltingly, however partially. In
contrast, the women who undergo plastic surgery are simply
making do within a culture that they believe judges and rewards
them for their looks.

CHAPTER FOUR

NAAFA

Reinterpreting the Fat Body

The last three chapters have examined women's attempts to ne-gotiate nondeviant identities within institutions organized around altering the body. Hairstyling, aerobics, and plastic surgery serve not only as methods for shaping women's appearances but also as techniques for neutralizing bodies that will never meet cultural standards for beauty. Furthermore, I have shown—particularly in the introduction and chapter 1—that women can create spaces of empowerment from within an oppressive system of beauty ideology while neither rejecting that ideology nor clearly chal-lenging it.

Importantly, hairstyling, aerobics, and plastic surgery involve body work aimed at changing minor, run-of-the-mill departures from ideal beauty—the wrinkled skin, unruly hair, and thick thighs that many women possess. In contrast, participants in NAAFA have bodies that fall outside this "normal" range, bod-ies that are sufficiently aberrant as to induce abusive remarks from friends and strangers, to make finding a job difficult or impossible, and to block individuals from ever experiencing anything close to "normal" lives.

The National Association to Advance Fat Acceptance was created explicitly to contest popular notions of beauty. It was established in 1969 as a nonprofit civil rights organization seeking "to increase the well-being of fat people."[1] NAAFA policy documents charge society with regarding its fat members as unsightly and undisciplined. According to NAAFA, members of the broader society attribute to fat people not only physical ugliness but also character flaws and immorality. As a result, NAAFA members argue, they are discriminated against socially and professionally; they are often unable to buy clothes, gain access to common spaces such as the theater and public transportation, or obtain health and life insurance. Fat people receive inferior treatment from health professionals and little understanding from their own families. They are frequently stared at and regularly victimized by tasteless jokes and verbal assaults. The result, according to the NAAFA home page, is often a poor self-image and feelings of worthlessness and guilt.[2]

NAAFA's stated goals include pursuing anti-size-discrimination legislation, assisting in litigation involving size discrimination, investigating negative treatment of fat people in educational policies and practices, and seeking more respectful medical care and better insurance coverage. NAAFA also sponsors social events like dances, parties, and dinners to put NAAFA members in contact with individuals who are attracted to fat people. Based on anecdotal evidence, NAAFA estimates that 5 to 10 percent of the population has a sexual preference for a fat partner. These individuals—who are almost exclusively men—are referred to within the organization as "Fat Admirers," or "FAs." While the social events are organized for NAAFA members, it is understood that FAs will attend the functions looking for fat women, many of whom, in turn, come to these events to meet men who view them as potential sexual partners. Indeed, the organization's social activities are the primary reason that many join the group.

Not unlike women who partake of hairstyling, aerobics, or plastic surgery, members of NAAFA use the organization to construct a normative identity by renegotiating the relationship of body and self. Within the group, this conceptualization takes two forms, both of which differ from that of the broader culture by dismissing the notion that the stigmatized body implies a flawed character. In the first instance, the organization argues that the fat body and the self are unrelated. NAAFA thus denies the traditional moral implications of the fat body, including laziness, low self-esteem, vice, and stupidity. In its attempts to create a safe, sexualized social environment for its membership, NAAFA also transforms the meanings of the fat body. In NAAFA social life, the fat body symbolizes a variety of positive identity traits, ranging from generosity to assertiveness to candid sensuality. Despite the group's considerable efforts, however, attempts to renegotiate self and body are limited in their success.

Reminiscent of Gresham Sykes and David Matza's discussion of "techniques of neutralization"—in which the authors point out that even the most strenuous efforts to negate the meaning of deviant acts may fail in the context of internalized values and the reactions of "conforming others"[3]—NAAFA's attempts to renegotiate meanings of the fat body rarely convert either outsiders or NAAFA members themselves. Because NAAFA exists in a world that unwaveringly links body to self—and, by implication, connects the stigmatized body to a flawed self—the organization is unable to offer its members successful techniques for neutralizing the failed body. As products of the culture in which they live, NAAFA members may attempt to renegotiate meanings of the fat body; however, they are able to do so only within the insulation of the organization's social life. They are still bombarded with and influenced by broader cultural understandings of the body, and they construct identities that are shaped by those understandings.

RESEARCH AND METHODS

I attended my first function with the local chapter of NAAFA in December 1992. I learned about the organization through a contact in my academic department who had conducted research in the group several years earlier. This contact, a male faculty member, told me to expect a hostile response from NAAFA's female members. He said that the group would likely react to me, an average-sized woman, as if I "should come back when [I had] gained a hundred pounds." As one member later explained to me, NAAFA women are suspicious of thin women in their group, fearing that they will compete for the scarce male resources that the organization offers (despite the fact that men attend NAAFA functions explicitly to meet women who are not thin). By her account, members believe that because FAs have learned to feel ashamed of their sexual preference for fat women, they will pursue a thin woman almost by reflex if one is present. A thin woman could theoretically attend NAAFA activities in hopes of meeting fat men. However, because the group is composed almost exclusively of fat women, it is unlikely that a heterosexual female FA would use the organization as a resource for her romantic pursuits.

I phoned the cochairs of the local chapter and explained my interest in the group. One of them, Sylvia, invited me to their up-coming Christmas party, at which thirty to forty guests were ex-pected.[4] I arrived earlier than most of the members and was able to discuss my reasons for wanting to study NAAFA with Sylvia and her boyfriend, Mark. Both accepted me warmly, welcoming me and my interest in the group. I explained to Sylvia and Karen, the second cochair, that I was very concerned that I not intrude in the group. They reassured me that my presence would not be a problem, claiming that if members did not wish to speak to me, they would let Sylvia or Karen know.

That December evening began my three years of participant-observation in NAAFA. Soon after the party, I became a member of the chapter and attended its business meetings, dinners (which were always held in all-you-can-eat restaurants), parties, dances, fashion shows, and clothing swaps. While I never en-countered the extent of hostility my colleague had warned me about, I often received questioning stares from individuals who did not know my purpose and brusque comments from mem-bers who did. At one of the first dinners I attended, I sat directly across from a fifty-five-year-old woman whose weight (between 400 and 450 pounds) and associated health problems confined her to a wheelchair. She asked why I was at the dinner, and I ex-plained that I was interested in the things women do to change their bodies. She responded by asking, "So, are we [fat women] your greatest fear?" "No," I answered, flustered. "You are the heroes of my work." Unfortunately, my response failed to satisfy the woman, who rarely spoke to me from that day forward.

During my research on NAAFA, I noticed that very few of the group's activities were politically oriented, despite the fact that NAAFA describes itself as a civil rights organization. I began to search out the more political end of NAAFA and soon learned through a women's studies network that the group's Fat Feminist Caucus (FFC) was holding a conference in a nearby state. I contacted the organizer of the group, explained that I was studying NAAFA as part of a research project, and asked if I might be permitted to attend. Hesitantly, she said that I could come, adding that I would be expected to introduce myself and explain my presence to conference participants.

Having decided to attend the convention, I was greeted there by the treasurer of the caucus, who insisted that I was in "the wrong place." When I explained who I was and that I had been given permission to attend, she grudgingly told me I could take a seat in the conference room but threatened me with expulsion if I acted "inappropriately."

The Fat Feminist Caucus conference provided me with my first glimpse into the political side of NAAFA. It also revealed quite clearly the organization's attempts to neutralize the body by (ideologically) severing it from selfhood. FFC members invest little time or energy in reshaping the meanings of or sexualizing the fat female body, as the local chapter does. Rather, as a group organized to assert the political rights of fat women, the FFC argues that fat is essentially meaningless and, by implication, has few ramifications for identity.

THE WOMEN OF NAAFA

Sylvia is a forty-five-year-old bookkeeper. She is 5 feet 8 inches tall, brunette, and around 350 pounds. A friendly person with a lively wit, Sylvia treats all members with warmth and caring, plans many of the group's social and political activities, and organizes much of her own life around her involvement in NAAFA. Obese even in early childhood, Sylvia recalls her experiences with weight. She told me that she was "fat from a little kid," describing herself as a "little, like, roly-poly." She explains, "I was 140 pounds in fifth grade and that was considered way too fat, but I was also 5 foot 6. In fifth grade that was considered too fat."

When she was ten, Sylvia's parents took her to a doctor for weight-loss therapy. The physician prescribed amphetamines, which Sylvia took for several months, and she lost a considerable amount of weight. Because the pills eventually began to make her faint, Sylvia stopped taking them around age eleven, at which point she gained "a tremendous amount of weight," all that she had lost and 20 percent more. By the time she entered junior high school, Sylvia weighed 200 pounds, where she remained for four years until, at age sixteen, she went to another diet doctor. That doctor not only prescribed oral stimulants, but also gave her amphetamine shots. She notes, "Years later, we found out it was speed...I lost 80 pounds."

Sylvia says that weight has affected nearly all aspects of her life, including her relationships with men and family members, education, and employment. She says, "I was accepted to three [nursing] schools and I knew I couldn't go to any of them because I had lied on the application, saying I was 180 pounds. That was the top weight that they would accept." Weighing 225 pounds, Sylvia knew that she would have to lose 45 pounds before the school physical, just three months away. Unable to reach 180 pounds, Sylvia instead attended the two-year nursing program at a local community college. While the program had no weight requirements, it provided training far inferior to that offered by the other three schools. She eventually became frustrated with the program and dropped out of college. For the next ten years, she worked in numerous odd jobs, eventually becoming a bookkeeper.

In addition to her struggles with weight and her educational and occupational challenges, Sylvia faced problems with her parents, who were, she says, "always my worst critics." Sylvia's mother, a secretary, had been slightly overweight in her teens but managed to become and remain slender. Her father, a construction foreman, was quite thin until he entered his sixties, after which he gained approximately 15 pounds. By her account, Sylvia's parents attempted to manage her eating behavior throughout her life. Her mother "became totally obsessed with trying to control [Sylvia's] body," to the point of monitoring the contents of all the food containers in the home. Sylvia says, "She would have everything marked. She'd know how many cookies were in every box. She would actually put little tick marks on the milk carton, so that if I drank a glass of milk, she would know that I had done that.... Eventually, it became this battle of wills of me trying to find more and more creative ways to actually get food." In Sylvia's recollection, her parents showed more or less affection for her depending on her eating behavior. She was required to lose weight "for the family, in order to...make them proud, to make them respectable. I was shaming the family by being fat. That's why I was good if I was going along with the program, and bad, unlovable, if I didn't."

Believing that her weight made her "unlovable," Sylvia's parents told her that she would never find a husband. Nevertheless, Sylvia married when she was twenty-one. Her husband, a successful engineer from an upper-middle-class family, had shocked Sylvia's parents by falling in love with her. She recalls that several months before her wedding, Sylvia's mother convinced her father to tell her, "'We don't think that you should wear white to your wedding.' I said, 'Why?' and he said, 'Well, because you're not a virgin,' and I said, 'You are so full of crap. Mom doesn't want me to wear white because it makes fat girls look fatter... well, I'm wearing anything I want.' So I cut my parents out of my wedding plans completely."

Sylvia's marriage ended after two years, during which time she gave birth to a daughter. Several years later, she received a telephone call from an old friend. Mary, who is also a fat woman, had gone through a Weight Watchers program with Sylvia, and together they had lost—and later regained—over 80 pounds each. Sylvia recalls the telephone conversation: "Mary goes, 'What are you doing?' I said, 'I have a three-year-old daughter and I'm sitting home on the weekends.' She said, 'Do I have a place for you! What if I told you there's a place you could go and dance and the men want to dance with you because you're fat?' I said, 'Right.'"

Despite Sylvia's initial hesitation, she decided to attend a NAAFA dance with her friend. "I never looked back. I embraced this thing totally." For the first time in her life, Sylvia found herself in a social group in which she was considered attractive because of her body rather than, at best, in spite of it. Even if only in a small, isolated group, Sylvia was recognized as a sexual person. The organization provided her with a sexual outlet, a place where she could pursue men openly without fear of rebuff of her stigmatized body.

Five years later, Sylvia met her current boyfriend, with whom she has now lived for three years. She explains that at the time she met Mark, her interactions in NAAFA had helped her come to terms with being fat, stop dieting, and feel that she was "a whole person" without a man in her life. Sylvia says,

> I made the conscious decision. Just like I didn't need to diet to be a real person, I didn't need to have a man in my life to be a happy person. Two months later I met him, you know.... He did enrich my life. He didn't come in and make it better... well, he made it better in ways, but I was already completely there. I was already a whole person.

Sylvia learned to see herself as "completely there," explicitly through her involvement in NAAFA.

Many of the members of NAAFA told me that before joining the organization, they had never been in a social group that had welcomed and accepted them. The women described childhood homes that provided little comfort: they were often chastised for their weight, tormented by their siblings, and neglected by their parents. For example, Terry, a thirty-four-year-old student and member of the local chapter, discussed numerous battles with her mother, who controlled her eating and punished her for not caring more about her appearance. She describes one revealing incident in her childhood:

> I couldn't find my bike. I ask my mom, and she says, "I gave your bicycle to the moving man. His little girl didn't have a bicycle," and I said, "Well, your little girl doesn't have a bicycle either, you idiot." We had this terrible fight. So finally she says to me, "I gave your bicycle away because I don't want the new neighbors seeing your fat ass riding up and down the block."

Terry's story resembles the experiences endured by many NAAFA members. Diane, a thirty-six-year-old receptionist, remembers her mother saying, "Opportunity only knocks once, and you'll be too fat to open the door." Diane says, "That's one of my favorite quotes, and, 'Don't bring any of your boyfriends home because we don't want to meet anybody that would date you.' Or, 'Men only date you because you have a car.'...These were words of wisdom, you know."

For many of these women, NAAFA becomes a new family. During one meeting of the Fat Feminist Caucus, much of the conversation focused on the importance of the group as an environment where the women's experiences of victimization were recognized, their feelings of need and loss validated. At this particular meeting, a first-time attendee tearfully spoke of her gratitude for a place where she could feel like she was "okay." Several other women said that they hated to think about "where [they] would be" without the group. Two others joked that they had to hold each other down because their happiness lifted them into the air.

In addition to having poor family relationships, many members of NAAFA remember having few friends while they were growing up. Many were teased incessantly, often to the point that they would skip school to avoid other children's ridicule. Terry recalls,

> I was brand-new to the neighborhood, and a guy in my
> French class would start yelling things about me being fat
> and making jokes and getting his buddies to all laugh with
> him, and I started sneaking into class early and getting way in
> the back, because we had these, like, booths....You sat there

with, you know, the earphones and stuff, and I knew if I
could get into the last row, then Philip wouldn't see me.

And Katherine, fifty-one years old, told me that she grew up feeling as if she had no place in which to feel sheltered or secure. She
"didn't feel safe in school" or "in the streets" or even when she went
home. Based on these experiences, Katherine says that she views
the world outside NAAFA as "basically threatening."

NAAFA provides its members with a safe harbor. It also becomes one of the only places where fat women are considered
sexual beings. Indeed, many of the women I interviewed told me
that they had never felt attached to their bodies as objects of sexual desire or attraction until they came to NAAFA. Tamara, a
thirty-two-year-old engineer and member of the FFC, told me
that she "had had a sense that [she] was a sexual being, but not really that [she's] a woman in a woman's body." Tamara went on to
explain that fat women separate themselves from their bodies because they, like other members of society, come to believe that
their appearance is unacceptable.

Before becoming involved in NAAFA, many of the group's
members had few romantic involvements; their interest in men
or boys was often ignored or even ridiculed. Sheila recalls a particularly humiliating experience: "When I was in third grade, I
told my girlfriend that I liked one of the little boys in class and
he caught up with me in the back of the school yard and punched
me in the arm and said, 'Don't you ever tell anybody you like
me,' you know, and I knew it was because I was the fat kid."
Others described themselves as being sexually disinterested before they encountered an environment that acknowledged them
as sexually attractive women. Amy, a twenty-eight-year-old stu-

dent and member of the FFC, told me that before learning about fat pride ideology, she had believed that her life would be void of sexuality. She described herself as having always been "neuter," and exclaimed her shock on first encountering men who sought her out as a sexual partner.

Many of the women said that even though they had been sexually active and romantically involved with men before entering NAAFA, their partners often criticized their bodies and showed them little respect. Karen told me that before joining NAAFA she had repeatedly involved herself with men who treated her cruelly. In one such instance, she discovered that her partner had been lying to her about his involvement with another woman. When she confronted the man about his lie, he said that she "was not attractive enough to tell the truth to."

Rose, a thirty-eight-year-old secretary and member of the local chapter, told me about a particularly sadistic man whom she lived with for nearly four years: "He said, 'I'd rather put my foot in a snake pit than make love to you'... 'Giagundus Woman' was like the nickname [he used]." She continued, "I'd do the laundry, and I'd say, 'Could you go take the stuff out of the washer and put it in the dryer?' He'd say, 'No, go downstairs and do it yourself. If you were thin, it wouldn't be a problem, you know. It's good for you.'" Rose left this man and became involved with her first "FA," who admired her fat body and respected her. Because the FA "didn't have much upstairs," however, their relationship soon ended.

NAAFA offers members a welcoming social environment, potential friends with similar experiences of size discrimination, and an opportunity for sexual and romantic pursuits. Within the organization, NAAFA women do not need to fear that their sexual interests will be ignored or, worse, despised. NAAFA members also gain access to seamstresses and clothing manufacturers who produce lingerie and evening wear for fat women, and they often "dress up" for the first time at the group's social events. Within NAAFA, fat women can flirt candidly, flaunt their sensuality, and openly pursue men without fear of disdain.

ALTERNATIVE ATTEMPTS
TO NEUTRALIZE THE BODY

NAAFA, an organization of stigmatized individuals, attempts to offer its members what Erving Goffman has called "advocated codes of conduct" for dealing with themselves and the "normal" world.[5] These codes provide members with alternative techniques for neutralizing the fat body and constructing normative identities. Within its formal doctrines and more informally in group interactions, NAAFA prescribes particular approaches to self and body. Specifically, NAAFA members come to the group to learn methods of dealing with the self that are more positive than those offered by the larger society. They seek out constructive ways of incorporating the stigmatized body into identity—of not equating a failed body with a flawed self. The political strand of the group argues that fat women are no different from "normals," while the local chapter links fatness to a specific conceptualization of self—the sexualized, feminized self. NAAFA thus conceptualizes the body-self relationship in two distinct—and somewhat contradictory—ways. This "self-contradiction,"[6] to use Goffman's terminology, means that for NAAFA members, the fat body is simultaneously the self and not the self.

Politics of Self and Body:
The Fat Feminist Caucus

The political segments of the organization see the self and body as separate entities. Time and time again in its formal statements, political activities, and member newsletters, NAAFA claims that the traditional moral implications of the fat body—including sloth, ignorance, and self-hatred—are not, in truth, associated with fat. NAAFA's members argue that they are as capable, intelligent, and worthy as average-sized members of the society and so should be granted equal rights and respect. Furthermore, with assurances that "it's not your fault that you're fat," NAAFA's literature claims that fat individuals are not personally responsible for their weight.[7] Instead, NAAFA cites medical literature pointing to the influence of genetic predisposition and the limits of restrictive dieting on body size.[8]

In this conceptualization, the fat body has no implications for identity. However, because society discriminates against fat people based on a single, effectively accidental, characteristic, the organization recommends specific tools for building self-esteem. These tools include facing "our whole, complete selves and loving all our parts, not just the nice sides but the complete package, 'warts' and all.... Take a good look at yourself, take stock, and begin to affirm what is good, and love and accept the rest."[9] According to NAAFA, fat people are just like everyone else. Their good qualities may include being "sensitive" and "responsible," while their bad ones might include being "controlling" or "spiteful."[10] While these negative characteristics may very well deserve assessment, self-esteem requires that they also be accepted. Critically, in NAAFA's formulation, these negative qualities do not include fatness. Fat is unrelated to identity; it is, therefore, not necessarily bad to be fat. Fat, according to the *NAAFA Workbook,* "is not a four-letter word."[11] In keeping with Goffman's argument, the group suggests that stigmatized individuals define themselves as "no different from any other human being," even as those around them define them as deviant.[12] Although the outside world may ascribe specific identities to fat persons, NAAFA members themselves contend that the self is independent of the body.

Among the groups I studied, attempts to conceptualize self and body as separate and distinct are particularly apparent in the work of the Fat Feminist Caucus. Group members rely on notions of the disembodied self as they negotiate their political activities and their individual attempts to come to terms with being fat. Women who come to this group (usually after they participate in one of NAAFA's local chapters or its national convention and dislike the sexualized environment) are primarily interested in political activity and community building rather than in romantic liaisons or a fat-centered social life. The Fat Feminist Caucus stresses that personal and political "empowerment" is possible through a shared understanding of each other's experiences and the bond of shared oppression.

At one of the group's conferences, its members focused on the topic "Ten Years: Where You've Been, How You've Changed, Where You're Going," discussing their experiences of being fat and the different methods they have used to come to terms with their stigmatized bodies. Three main themes emerged during the discussion: the women's attempts to find support, validation, and connection within the group; their struggles to come to terms with being fat; and their efforts to defend themselves against fat discrimination and share their experiences. In essence, all dealt

with techniques for constructing nondeviant identities acceptable to both themselves and "normals."

FFC members are, on the whole, much fatter than women in
the local NAAFA chapter. They are also more articulate and, it
seems to me, more insightful. As an almost entirely college-
educated group, many of whom have advanced degrees, the group
members have gained access to a feminist rhetoric; they use it to
fuel their indictments of fat discrimination and to come to terms
with their bodies. In many instances, the group's members distinguish "inner work" (coming to terms with being fat) from "outer
work" (making society more hospitable to fat people). While one
of these goals is personal and the other political, the two purposes
are linked. Candace, the caucus treasurer, says that while she was
once so ashamed of being fat that "you could control me with the
word 'fat,'" she no longer lives in fear of the criticism of onlookers. She says that she now uses the term "fat" to further her own
feminist agenda, speaking it freely to show that it has no implications for self-esteem or political entitlement. As Candace observes,
the personal work that FFC women do to accept being fat becomes enmeshed in their political activities, and, in turn, their political agendas become a means for neutralizing deviant bodies.

The Fat Feminist Caucus is organized around political action;
as something of a side effect, the group's members use their public projects to fuel their efforts to come to terms with their fat
bodies. Samantha, a forty-three-year-old college administrator
and member of the FFC, told me that through her participation
in groups like the caucus, she has both forced herself to accept
the physical space her body requires and learned to use her fat
body to make a statement about women's issues. Samantha says
that she has identified a "purpose" for her body: to further the

cause of women's political concerns. Linking her own struggles to those of women more generally, she has come to reconceptualize the relationship of body and identity. No longer living "from her neck down," Samantha explains that she has learned to experience a "physical life, a physical space," by accepting her body and the space it requires.

Being fat does not mean, for this group, that they have particular personality characteristics, positive or negative. Instead, the women assert that they are merely "as good" as others and, as such, deserve equal rights and equal access to educational and occupational opportunities. Many of the NAAFA women I interviewed, especially the largest ones, were unemployed or underemployed given their education and training. NAAFA contends that size discrimination is often to blame for its members' underemployment. In response, the organization has been involved in numerous weight-related employment discrimination lawsuits.

Few laws protect Americans from weight discrimination. Only one state, Michigan, includes the word "weight" in its civil rights legislation. Local statutes include an ordinance in Santa Cruz, California, that prohibits discrimination in employment, housing, and public accommodations based on physical charateristics, and an ordinance in Washington, D.C., that forbids discrimination based on appearance. A federal law, under Section 504 of the Rehabilitation Act of 1973, may serve to protect fat individuals from discrimination in the workplace. This law guarantees employment opportunities to anyone who is physically or mentally impaired. As defined, physical impairment includes disorder, loss, or disfigurement affecting one or more bodily systems. While this law does not refer directly to weight, it covers the mobility problems that many of NAAFA's largest members experience.[13]

NAAFA suggests various job strategies to its members. Members are urged to contact their fat friends to explore the attitudes toward weight and the availability of employment in their workplaces. NAAFA becomes a resource for employment in that its members serve as a network of information about fat-friendly organizations. The *NAAFA Workbook* offers its members detailed guidelines for making contacts and gathering information about employment possibilities. Members of NAAFA assume that the most difficult part of finding a job is surviving the first interview, because this is the point at which potential employers discover the applicant's stigma and begin to make assumptions about personality and work performance. Again, the *NAAFA Workbook* guides its members through the process, suggesting that "the only way to combat size discrimination...[is to take] the bull by the horns and address the weight issue in the most positive way possible."[14] Specifically, NAAFA members are urged to introduce the topic of weight, point out that size has never negatively affected their performance, suggest that they may actually work harder and better than their colleagues just to feel accepted, and mention that they will be loyal to the employer because jobs are harder for fat people to find. The *NAAFA Workbook* adds that the applicant should ask her potential employer to contact her references, since these people will assure the interviewer that her past work has been excellent.

In another example of size discrimination, NAAFA women point to limited access to amenities. Buses, planes, schools, theaters, and restaurants often fail to provide fat people with seats that can accommodate their large bodies. As a result, the women I interviewed often avoid these places or force themselves to request larger chairs. Amy says that she cannot sit in university chairs, at least not if she wants to be "comfortable enough to take notes." But she explains, "I've gotten up the nerve to ask for a larger chair to be brought in, and Student Services will do it, but they won't do it unless I remind them before every class. It's irritating."

Amy considers her attempts to obtain adequate seating akin to a political and personal triumph. Resisting her university's tendency to ignore the needs of fat people, she is defending herself and her "community." The *NAAFA Workbook* refers to such action as refusing to do the "fat shuffle."[15] This term, derived from the self-deprecating behavior once associated with oppressed American Blacks, includes the excuses and rationalizations fat people use to avoid "unpleasantness and embarrassment," like telling friends that they are "too sick or busy to join them, when the truth is you don't have the appropriate clothing"; sitting "in your car outside the store waiting for the group of teenagers who might taunt you to disperse"; and "avoiding public places, public transportation, and eating in public."[16] NAAFA asks its members to recognize the ways they "shuffle" and to choose instead to stand their ground. Again, NAAFA provides its members with a resource for personal strength, with a reason for refusing to be victimized.

NAAFA argues that many fat people are unable to find adequate medical services. Most of the women I interviewed discussed discrimination from physicians who refuse to treat them for even the simplest of illnesses unless they lose weight. A female member says that she once went to a physician for a prescription for oral contraceptives, only to have him exclaim, "*You* need birth control?" Another went to a doctor to get a decongestant. When she walked into his office, he said, "I won't give you anything until you lose fifty pounds." She responded, "I just want some fucking cold medicine, what does that have to do with my weight?" She left without waiting for his response.

Despite the behavior of outsiders, NAAFA ideology holds that members are not fat because of their eating behaviors but as a result of genetic propensities to overweight and low metabolism resulting from a lifetime of restrictive dieting. Members of NAAFA, therefore, are not themselves responsible for being fat (and thus they are not worthless, undisciplined, or slothful), and so they deserve medical care that is sensitive to the special needs of fat people rather than doctors who blame them for their weight and force them to diet. Charging that restrictive dieting only makes fat people fatter, NAAFA gives its members reasons to avoid what it considers to be self-destructive behavior.

Even though NAAFA does not openly condemn dieting, the organization does state that attempts to lose weight through restricted eating are rarely successful. Moreover, the group's ideology implies that individuals who attempt to lose weight are unable to accept themselves totally. With regard to medical treatment, NAAFA literature suggests that its members phone doctors before visiting their offices, in order to avoid embarrassing confrontations and wasted time.[17] Finally, NAAFA reminds its members that "you are the customers" and, as such, have the freedom to refuse medical treatment from prejudiced physicians.

In response to the social criticism and cultural meanings of fat, many NAAFA women have told me that they have learned to detach self from body, thereby perceiving their bodies as separate from "who they really are." While it is unlikely that the FFC would purport a dissociation of self and body at the individual level, differentiating the person from the negative social meanings of the fat body clearly serves the group's ideological and political purposes. However, NAAFA members themselves say that they find the severing of self from body to be personally destructive. For example, Moira, a thirty-year-old member of the local chapter, told me that she reacts to ridicule by "withdrawing from my skin, like I'm not going to be part of my physical body anymore." She dissociates self and body because she needs "to be detached from the object of all that hatred." Moreover, she tries to be "in my mind, someone else so fascinating that I wouldn't even need to have a body, so my body wouldn't matter." At the same time, Moira says that her attempts to uncouple the body and self are ultimately "utterly destructive," because "it is a rejection of part of me....I am a fat woman. I would rather not have to live in a sort of fantasy world where I am only part of who I am." Moira—much like other members of NAAFA—has learned to survive in a hostile social environment by coming to see her body as essentially not who she is. However, denying the physical part of her entity is unsatisfying to Moira because it feels inauthentic.

In a recent survey, NAAFA found that 51 percent of its membership has experienced weight-related job discrimination.[18] From this figure, it is easy to surmise that the disassociation of self and body purported by groups like NAAFA's Fat Feminist Caucus is not easily transferred to the broader society. Likely because of the group's limited size and scope as well as a general resistance to its message, the FFC's efforts to neutralize stigma meet with limited success. Meanings of the stigmatized body are clearly difficult to displace because self and body, at least in mainstream American culture, are too closely linked. In the end, even if NAAFA's members can construct identities independent of their bodies, the broader culture continues to discriminate against them.

Fat and Beautiful: The Local Chapter

The local chapter of NAAFA uses an alternative strategy for neutralizing the deviant body. This strand of the organization, rather than conceptualizing the self and body as distinct, instead attempts to transform the meaning of the fat body and, by implication, its significance for self. The men who come to NAAFA dances and parties come specifically to meet fat women. As other authors have commented, it is the fattest of the NAAFA women who are most highly prized and sought after by FAs.[19] In the economy of NAAFA social life, the fat body is a valuable resource. Specifically, NAAFA literature describes fat women in terms such as "majestic," "powerful," "complete," "sensual," and "feminine."[20] The fat woman is not weak or submissive; like her rebellious fat, she herself is "sassy, impertinent, disobedient."[21] And all of these characteristics are sexualized within NAAFA so that the fat body becomes an indicator of a strong, attractive, sexual, and feminine self. The character implications of the fat body are positive, as are its ramifications for identity. In this conceptualization, the fat body is highly indicative of the self.

NAAFA's reformulation of the meanings of the fat body is evident in the group's social activities. One evening in April 1993, I attended the chapter's spring dance and lingerie fashion show at the Knights of Columbus Hall in a nearby Long Island town. I had persuaded a male friend to attend with me, hoping that his presence would allay the members' fears of me as a potential competitor for male attention. We arrived at the dance early. There were only about fifty people present, with the women outnumbering the men by more than three to one. The number of both women and men increased to about 150 during the evening and the ratio evened out somewhat, to about two to one. When I arrived, most of the women were dancing with other women, some in groups of three or more and others in (nontouching, apparently heterosexual) female couples. During slow dances, there were only male-female couples on the floor. As the night progressed and more men arrived, mixed-gender couples started fast dancing, though many women still danced together in groups. During slow dances, couples often kissed. The DJ (a member of the musical group Bopping with the Big Boys) played a repertoire of songs about the beauty and sexual attractiveness of women.

The women's clothing ranged from moderately casual sweaters and large shirts, paired with leggings, miniskirts with tights or lacy hose, dressy shorts, and casual pants to very dressy dresses and sheer pantsuits (one woman's shirt was opaque only at her breasts), with plunging necklines that revealed considerable cleavage and sometimes even breast tattoos, layers of chiffon, and clinging dresses with spaghetti straps. On the whole, the women's clothes were quite revealing—short, tight, or low-cut—and were clearly intended to show off every bulge, roll, and jiggle. The members of NAAFA reveled in their fat, showing off their flesh to an audience that would, presumably, appreciate it. The women's positive attitudes about themselves and their appearances were obvious from their efforts to call attention to their bodies. Sarah, a woman with shoulder-length, bleached-blonde hair (and weighing about 200 pounds at 5 feet 5 inches) was wearing a red leather jacket and very tight red leather pants with six-inch red leather pumps. And Rebecca, a forty-six-year-old member with bleached-blonde hair (weighing around 230 pounds at 5 feet 4 inches), wore a sheer black shirt with long, full sleeves. Over her breasts, the shirt was a stretchy knit tied in the middle. Her pants were also a black stretch fabric, and the shirt hung down over them. She was wearing high-heeled black sandals and a great deal of makeup.

At 1:00 A.M., the dance floor was cleared for the fashion show, featuring clothes by a local seamstress who sells moderately priced apparel for fat women. The clothes ranged from wildly colorful tie-dyed jumpsuits to rayon and knit two-piece outfits of loosely fitting pants and flowing shirts, bell-bottom pants with oversized shirts, double-breasted business suits, dresses in bright red or orange for dinner or work, very dressy sequined dresses, and knit dresses with long fringes on the bottom. There were also a bridal dress and tuxedo modeled by a couple who had recently been married. The woman who made these clothes described each item, usually making a comment about the new styles now available to the "full-figured." After the regular clothes had been displayed, the lingerie and sleepwear portion of the show started. These clothes ranged from typical pajamas to completely sheer red nighties, "upstairs maid" fantasy teddies, a see-through outfit of a red camisole and tap pants, and a sheer white nightgown and robe. The outfits were modeled by NAAFA women who had been dancing with their friends just moments before; most left little of their bodies to the imagination. Judging by the catcalls in the crowd, all of the lingerie—and by association, the women's bodies and their candid sexuality—was accepted with enthusiasm.

Perhaps because of its overtly sexual theme, the spring dance seemed the most raucous of the NAAFA functions I attended. Members and guests were drinking and laughing into the small hours of the morning, and a general feeling of camaraderie pervaded the evening. The dance provided a glimpse of NAAFA's idealization and sexualization of fat. At least in this isolated setting, NAAFA members could embrace their bodies as objects of sexual desire and enjoy the ramifications that being desired has on their understanding of themselves. At this level of the organization and within this insulated space, the meaning of the fat body is transformed.

Importantly, the group's capacity to renegotiate understandings of fat is dependent on its ability to separate itself from the broader cultural significance of NAAFA members' stigmatized bodies. However, even in such a setting, participants are aware that their fat bodies—or their attraction to fat bodies—deviate from mainstream understandings of the significance of fat. When the fashion portion of the evening began, Sylvia announced that the show would be videotaped for a local television station. When I asked her why she had made the announcement, she responded that many of the FAs would want to leave the dance rather than risk being seen on television. Clearly, the men recognize that the safety of NAAFA social life, as well as the organization's ability to construct its own understandings of the fat female body, relies on the group's separation from the broader culture. They realize that the group appears markedly deviant to the outside world. In turn, the organization recognizes many FAs' desire to hide their attraction to fat people. NAAFA's literature suggests that societal, peer, and parental pressure may lead some FAs to stay "in the closet" about their preference rather than face the ridicule it would engender.

Members of NAAFA attempt to negotiate self and body in a culture that equates fat with disease, sin, ugliness, and even crime. And this negative identifier has obvious ramifications for both the character attributions of others and the negative attributions to self. In light of enormous social pressure to the contrary, NAAFA members are predictably unable to sustain at an individual level the group's particular understandings of the fat body or its implications for identity construction. At least at the cultural level, the body and self are too profoundly linked.

WHERE IT FAILS

While the two strands of NAAFA—the FFC and the local chapter—approach the relationship of self and body somewhat differently, both strategies aim to reduce the negative implications of the fat body. However, even though the group attempts to reconceptualize fat, few of the NAAFA women I interviewed perceive fat as attractive or desirable. Although many of the fat women longed to be involved in intimate relationships with men who appreciated them physically, none were involved romantically with fat men. Moreover, this lack of sexual interest in fat men suggests something of a disingenuousness on the women's part: they want to be considered sexual beings but do not see fat men in the same way. Furthermore, over half of the women I interviewed were, despite innumerable failed attempts, trying to lose weight, often at the same time that they criticized others' (and even their own) attempts to do so. NAAFA provides reasons for its members to stop dieting, arguing that the behavior is destined to failure and so hints at self-deception. While many of the women I interviewed recognize NAAFA's "party line" as valid, they nevertheless provide counterarguments, most commonly in the form of reasons why specific efforts to lose weight have proved unsuccessful. More than half of these women told me that their past diets failed primarily because they required unrealistic eating regimens; they were too restrictive of calories or food varieties, relied on drug treatment instead of behavior modification, or occurred at a time when the women were not, for some personal reason, "ready" to lose weight. Despite NAAFA's argument that fat people are fat because of genetic predisposition, the women often blamed specific—but not all—diets for their failure to lose weight.

In one typical example, Liz, a fifty-six-year-old seamstress and member of the local NAAFA chapter, told me that she had recently visited a doctor who diagnosed her with a blood disorder caused by the presence of yeast cells. On receiving this information, Liz began a diet free of fermented food products and lost weight. Another member of the local chapter told me that she had recently discovered a low-fat eating plan that allowed her to lose weight without cutting back excessively on calories. In these cases and others, members suggest that new diet programs or medical evidence will provide them with a means of losing weight. They are thus able to continue dieting and still subscribe, at least in part, to NAAFA ideology. That is, these members contend that most diets are unrealistic and doomed to failure, while hoping that they have finally found the one plan that will work for them.

Even though many NAAFA members are trying to lose weight, most regard being thin, or even being average sized, as attempting to "pass" as normal.[22] Many NAAFA women have experienced short periods of being at average weight. Most achieved the weight loss through drastic measures like liquid diets, fasting, diet pills, or gastric bypass surgery, and all gained at least as much weight back as they had lost. Importantly, all of them say that they were not truly "themselves" during these periods of thinness; they behaved in ways that they would not normally behave, were sexually promiscuous, acted haughty, and treated fat people unkindly. Describing herself when she was slim, Sylvia says, "Man, I thought my shit didn't stink. I was another person." And Terry recalls, "When I got thin, I would go out to bars and pick up guys. I had never been promiscuous before." They now suggest that they feel ashamed both for their behavior and for deluding themselves that they could "pass." And still, members of NAAFA continue to invest enormous amounts of time and energy in ridding themselves of their fat.

Although they may welcome sexual attention, few of the women in NAAFA trust or respect FAs. Most are suspicious of the men's motives and accuse them of pursuing fat women because they are looking for "mommies," need to feel physically overpowered, or are so insecure with their own attractiveness that they imagine that only fat women are desperate enough to date them.

NAAFA members often told me that they were not entirely comfortable with the fact that men in NAAFA regard them as attractive because of their body types. Not unlike other women who feel that they are valued solely for their appearance, NAAFA women resent FAs' attraction to a body "type" rather than to their emotional, physical, and intellectual traits. Many NAAFA members dislike the association of their fat bodies with particular—primarily sexual—characteristics. They question both the attachment of fat to sexual desirability (and, perhaps, sexual appetite) and the men who find them sexually attractive. In effect, they reject local NAAFA's transformation of the meaning of fat.

Even the members of NAAFA, then, fail to accept the organization's reconceptualizations of fat. Instead, these women continue to regard the fat body as significant for self and consider the stigmatized body as indicative of a self that is in some way flawed. Evidence for this failure lies in members' continued attempts to change their bodies, their rejection of fat men as sexual partners, and their scorn for FAs. Put succinctly, NAAFA members (just like the rest of the society) hate fat.

CONCLUSION

The literature on deviance disavowal has repeatedly shown that techniques aimed at neutralizing norm violation meet with varying degrees of success. In one study, Michael Benson examined thirty white-collar offenders' attempts to defeat the degradation ceremonies involved in criminal adjudication.[23] Benson shows that these criminals for the most part successfully deny criminality through the use of accounts. Most offenders interviewed acknowledge that their behavior can be construed as illegal, but they uniformly deny that it is motivated by what Benson calls "the guilty mind," or conscious criminal intent.[24] In other words, these individuals manage to admit to wrongdoing without conceptualizing themselves as wrongdoers. In this way, they construct nondeviant identities without denying criminal action.

In a contrasting study of the stigma of divorce, Naomi Gerstel shows that despite evidence that divorce is becoming less stigmatized (such as rising divorce rates and relaxation of church and state controls), the divorced themselves continue to feel devalued.[25] They think of themselves as "failures" and, more often than not, reject institutionalized contact (such as self-help groups) with others who are divorced.[26] Even when they do join such groups, they are likely to argue that their involvement is intended to benefit their children rather than themselves. Furthermore, in both their talk and action, the divorced reveal a commitment to the idea that being married is "normal." In so doing, they effectively legitimize their own stigmatization.[27]

Such examples suggest that individuals' attempts to negotiate normative identities are not always successful, particularly if they are stigmatized.[28] Throughout this book, I have argued that body work, at least in the four sites I have studied, is a means by which women attempt to construct nondeviant identities despite imperfect bodies. While NAAFA is one example of female work on the body, its members clearly stand apart from the inhabitants of Pamela's Hair Salon, John Norris's surgical clinic, or Long Island aerobics studios because NAAFA women's bodies prohibit them from living "normal" lives. That is, the bodies NAAFA women inhabit not only deviate from the cultural ideal, they deviate strikingly even from the "failed" bodies that most women have.

Because of this difference, NAAFA, more explicitly that hairstyling, aerobics, or plastic surgery, provides empirical evidence for the limits of women's capacity to negotiate nondeviant identities in light of deviant bodies. Not unlike Gerstel's divorcees, women in NAAFA devalue their own condition by refusing to date fat men, rejecting Fat Admirers, and continuing to try to lose weight. Essentially, the women in NAAFA spurn fellow members of their stigmatized group. In so doing, they reinforce rather than undermine the cultural fear and repudiation of fat.

Conclusion
The Body, Oppression, and Resistance

The body is a site of oppression, not only because physically stronger individuals can overpower weaker ones but also because systems of social control operate through it. I do not mean to imply that physicality in itself is oppressive, but instead that the body serves as a symbol of social difference and a basis for discrimination. In a society that equates the body with both self and moral worth, cultural meanings are attached to physical differences, so that the body provides a foundation for oppression based on gender, class, ethnicity, and age—all social characteristics that are deeply embodied.

Although this work has focused primarily on women's responses to beauty ideology, I now turn to a discussion of ideological control, particularly as it is revealed in the institutional enactment of body work and the accounts women provide about their bodies. Within local institutional settings, women learn to enact gender, social class, ethnicity, and age through the body. They become aware of the rules governing such enactment as well as the consequences of defying them. Women learn that these institutions offer remedies for many of the markers of, for example, aging, ethnicity, and even womanhood. While this process may not introduce the notion that such characteristics undermine social worth, it surely reinforces the idea. Furthermore, women discover that the definition of physical perfection is ever-changing, so that they must be constantly vigilant in their self-examination, always searching for methods of correction.

In the cosmetic surgery clinic, women learn that the medical industry can provide remedies for the hooked or wide noses and the almond-shaped eyes that indicate ethnicity. Prior to entering the physician's office, women are undoubtedly aware that such features are considered "defects"; however, it is only in the clinic that they become aware of modern medicine's techniques for solving their "problems." Cosmetic surgery can also repair the signs of aging with face-lifts and eye-lifts and the markers of childbearing with tummy tucks and breast alterations. Moreover, surgery not only corrects physical flaws; it can also, according to one of John Norris's advertisements, provide the opportunity to "look like the person you really are." The medical industry thus provides a means of enacting normative identity, of becoming the youthful "WASP" who is the only truly valued member of contemporary Western culture. In the very act of correction, the surgical practice effectively locates other body types within the realm of the deviant.

Not unlike the surgical clinic, the hair salon defines women's physical flaws according to the remedies that it makes available. As one example, hairstylists try to convince their clients to undergo procedures (such as hair coloring) that will diminish the signs of aging and allow them to convey an image of youthfulness, even if clients have "no idea how badly [they] need…it." The "need" refers to the requirements of a youthful appearance, insofar as "youth" is defined through hair color. Even though the stylist quoted is somewhat baffled by her client's refusal to color her gray hair, she does not educate her about its association with old age or, more important, its suggestion that the client is ignorant of beauty standards. The hairdresser's role as a service provider and her dependence on her clientele's loyalty limit her ability to spell out the connotations of gray hair. Nevertheless, when she urges her client to "wash away the gray," the stylist makes it clear that the client should camouflage the indicators of her true age. In the same way, salon customers learn that only particular hairstyles are acceptable for older women. Less "sexy" styles, according to one client, enable women to be feminine in an "appropriate" way for their particular age. Within the salon, clients also learn to distinguish their own appearance from that of their working-class beauticians. Customers develop a sense of what sorts of physical displays to avoid (such as frequently changing hair color) as well as what styles (such as "natural-looking" hair) are suitable to their own social status. The meanings of appropriate gender enactment are at least partly constructed and undoubtedly reinforced within the salon. While these meanings may vary according to the social class and ethnicity of the salon inhabitants, my research indicates that the salon provides an arena for the dissemination of both age- and class-appropriate standards of appearance and an understanding of the identity implications of appearance.

In aerobics classes, women come to understand that their bodies are flawed in ways that they may not have previously recognized. By following the teacher's instructions, women learn to focus on their "trouble spots"; they become aware of those spots as they progress through a series of exercises intended to "tone" buttocks, hips, inner thighs, and abdomen. Identifying such feminine parts of the body as "trouble" both reinforces the notion that the female body is, by definition, imperfect (despite women's efforts to the contrary) and underscores the body's inability to convey an unproblematic identity. In addition, although participants often use aerobics to suit their own purposes, one could reasonably argue that the classes themselves focus members' attention on the gaze of others rather than on the activity itself or the physical sensations that it generates. That is, because the gym's aerobics studio provides visual access (through a glass wall in the back of the room) to other gym members, class participation necessarily becomes a performance and, as such, mirrors women's experiences outside the class. In addition, while the mirrors on the front and side walls allow some women to acknowledge their own and other members' accomplishments, they reinforce the importance of improving appearance. By reflecting the gazes of onlookers, the mirrors make it difficult for class members to forget that they are being watched by reminding them that they must constantly monitor the movement and appearance of their bodies. In essence, the design of the aerobics studios heightens participants' awareness of self as object.

Even NAAFA, at least at the local level, supports gender oppression by creating an environment for the sexual objectification of women. Although the chapter provides its members with an arena in which to enact sexuality, it does so by defining women almost exclusively in terms of their weight. NAAFA members are positioned as no more than a body type, as opposed to a rich and complex intermingling of emotional, intellectual, *and* physical traits, so that relationships with the men who come to NAAFA functions often fail to provide members with the intimacy they long for. Nevertheless, many NAAFA members continue to involve themselves with "Fat Admirers," whom they may neither like nor respect, because they fear that they have no other options.

While systems of oppression based on gender, social class, age, and ethnicity operate through institutions of body work and serve to construct the body and its meanings, these groups simultaneously provide a conceptual space in which women may resist the demands of beauty ideology. For example, women respond to the demands of the hair salon with appeals to higher loyalties like motherhood and employment. As occupants of a female institution, representatives of the hair salon recognize and validate such appeals. Stylists use work on the body and their own understandings of hair and appearance to position themselves as professionals with specialized knowledge and skills in order to nullify the social differences between themselves and their customers.

Women in aerobics draw from that institution a concept of themselves that relies largely on nonphysical characteristics. In so doing, they neutralize the body as an indicator of self by reducing the moral significance of flawed bodies in favor of the more positive indicators of strength, capability, and determination. By diminishing the importance of appearance, the aerobics participants are also able to construct accounts of their bodies that position them as accidents and limit personal responsibility for them.

Even plastic surgery, a seemingly extreme form of physical invasion, becomes for John Norris's patients a method of detaching selfhood from the "flawed" body. As part of their efforts to escape the specter of inauthenticity associated with plastic surgery, the women come to understand their preoperative body as accidental and their current, more "normative" appearance as a more accurate indicator of who they truly are.

Body work is not only a resource for resistance; it is also a source of pleasure involving physicality, sexuality, and activity. For instance, in the aerobics classes, women learn to admire the strength of their bodies and their physical accomplishments. They no longer feel physically inadequate compared to culturally idealized bodies but can instead focus on their own stamina and muscularity, which they find empowering. Women in the hair salon frequently describe the sensual pleasure they experience while having their hair washed and styled, their nails painted, and their makeup applied. In fact, one client describes the salon as her "favorite place in the world" and another as the only place she can "relax and be pampered." Clearly, in both sites, women revel in the physical sensations of body work. At least in these instances, they seem to experience body work as a source of pleasure, rather than a form of domination.

Body work also allows women to develop their sexual identities and enhance sexual pleasure. Many of the women who underwent cosmetic surgery told me that they did so to experience both their bodies and sexual activity as more satisfying and pleasing. Frequently, these women explained that dissatisfaction with their preoperative bodies prohibited them from enjoying sex or feeling sexy. A woman who underwent abdominal liposuction says, "I have hated my tummy for sixteen years....It has affected me sexually." She explains that before having her abdomen reduced, she always felt too distracted by this "flaw" to fully enjoy sexual activity: "Who wants to be worrying about holding [her stomach] in during sex? Now I don't have to." Changing her body with cosmetic surgery permitted this woman to focus less on her appearance during sex and to more thoroughly enjoy the activity itself.

Finally, women who engage in body work often enjoy the work itself. For instance, the women in aerobics say that the rowdy, unladylike atmosphere in the aerobics studio helps them to relax. Yelling, stomping, and clapping, the class members are able, as one woman claims, to let themselves go. In a somewhat different sense, many women report that their favorite aspect of body work is interacting with other women in a predominantly female arena. For example, members of the Fat Feminist Caucus gain courage from sharing their experiences of oppression while also garnering strength from exchanging advice and comfort. In the hair salon and the aerobics studio, women are able to interact almost exclusively with other women and to discuss issues considered typically "female," like childbirth and child rearing, weddings and clothing, without embarrassment. Clearly, the women gain more from these sites of body work than merely some muscle tone, a good haircut, or manicured nails.

Although it would be gratifying to conclude this study with a claim that women who participate in body work are each day freer from the domination of beauty ideology, that would be a drastic overstatement. It is clear that women create pockets of resistance and derive some pleasure from these institutions. Nevertheless, their actions do not undermine the oppressive power of beauty ideals. Indeed, within these four organizations, I have uncovered resources for limited, rather than unqualified, female resistance. These limitations emerge from the very systems of gender, social class, ethnic, and age domination that operate through the body itself.

By reinforcing bases for class distinctions in appearance, the beauty ideology of the hair salon ensures that high-status women continue to distinguish themselves from those of lower status. Here, beauty ideology drives a wedge between groups of women: not, as one author has claimed, between the physically fit and unfit, but instead between those whose appearances indicate middle- or upper-class identities and those whose appearances indicate a lower social status.[1] The benefits of aerobics are undermined by the fact that members can "forgive" their flawed bodies only if they continue to attend classes regularly. When women miss more than a few classes, they become less able to ignore the moral meanings of the imperfect body or to focus on alternative indicators of self, such as accomplishments in work, education, or relationships. Similarly, while women who undergo cosmetic surgery may very well detach the "failed" body from the self, they do so at the price of an inauthenticity that requires considerable energy to alleviate—and which even then is never entirely extinguished. And although NAAFA may help fat women renegotiate the meanings of appearance, it does so successfully only within the very isolated sphere of the group itself.

Meanings of the body and self, resources for individual negotiation of meanings, and limitations on these negotiations are all mediated by the structures of institutions like the four I have described here. While some feminist writers have argued that the pressures of beauty ideology ensure that women construct negative images of self, my work has shown that such claims neglect structural resources and restraints—the organizational tenets, group forces, and commercial concerns—that, just like culture, mediate processes of identity construction. The failure of previous work to consider the structures of institutions in which meanings of the body and self are shaped has led to erroneous assumptions concerning meanings of the body. An undifferentiated analysis of culture has inclined observers to claim that beauty ideology is monolithic in its power to control women's aspirations concerning body and self. By examining the institutions in which beauty ideology operates and the individuals who react to that ideology, I show that structures shape these interactions by simultaneously enabling and limiting women's ability to carve out spaces of autonomy in which to shape their own meanings of self and body. A rigidly cultural—as opposed to structural—analysis of body work makes the activity appear to be an end in itself. The body might be a location of domination, but it is also a tool for resistance and agency in the construction and reconstruction of contemporary selfhood.

NOTES

INTRODUCTION

1. To preserve the anonymity of participants, all names are pseudonyms.

2. See Jane Rachael Kaplan, *A Woman's Conflict: The Special Relationship between Woman and Food* (Englewood Cliffs, N.J.: Prentice-Hall, 1980); Peter E. S. Freund, *The Civilized Body: Social Domination, Control, and Health* (Philadelphia: Temple University Press, 1982); John O'Neill, *Five Bodies: The Human Shape of Modern Society* (Ithaca: Cornell University Press, 1987); Emily Martin, *The Woman in the Body: A Cultural Analysis of Reproduction* (Boston: Beacon Press, 1992); Gerald McKnight, *The Skin Game: The International Beauty Business Brutally Exposed* (London: Sidgwick and Jackson, 1989); Mimi Nitcher and Nancy Vuckovic, "Fat Talk: Body Image among Adolescent Girls," in *Many Mirrors: Body Image and Social Relations,* ed. N. Sault (New Brunswick, N.J.: Rutgers University Press, 1994), 109–31; Becky W. Thompson, *A Hunger So Wide and So Deep: American Women Speak Out*

on Eating Problems (Minneapolis: University of Minnesota Press, 1994); Catherine Valentine, "Female Bodily Perfection and the Divided Self," in *Ideals of Feminine Beauty: Philosophical, Social, and Cultural Dimensions,* ed. K. Callaghan (Westport, Conn.: Greenwood Press, 1994), 113–24; Mary G. Winkler and Letha B. Cole, *Good Body: Asceticism in Contemporary Culture* (New Haven: Yale University Press, 1994); Arthur W. Frank, "Bringing Bodies Back In: A Decade Review," *Theory, Culture, and Society* 7 (1990): 131–62; Elizabeth Grosz, *Volatile Bodies: Toward a Corporeal Feminism* (Bloomington: Indiana University Press, 1994); Elizabeth Grosz and Elspeth Probyn, eds., *Sexy Bodies: The Strange Carnalities of Feminism* (London: Routledge, 1995); Pamela L. Moore, "Feminist Bodybuilding, Sex, and the Interruption of Investigative Knowledge," in *Building Bodies,* ed. Pamela L. Moore (New Brunswick, N.J.: Rutgers University Press, 1997), 74–86; Anne Bolin, "Flex Appeal, Food, and Fat: Competitive Bodybuilding, Gender, and Diet," in Moore, *Building Bodies,* 184–208; Lynda Goldstein, "Singing the Body Electric: Buying into Pop Cult Bodies," in Moore, *Building Bodies,* 209–16; Kathy Peiss, *Hope in a Jar* (New York: Metropolitan Books, 1998).

3. See Susan Bordo, "The Body and the Reproduction of Femininity: A Feminist Appropriation of Foucault," in *Gender/Body/Knowledge: Feminist Reconstructions of Being and Knowing,* ed. A. M. Jaggar and S. R. Bordo (New Brunswick, N.J.: Rutgers University Press, 1989), 13.

4. On the body and gender display, see Gerald R. Adams, "Physical Attributes, Personality Characteristics, and Social Behavior: An Investigation of the Effects of the Physical Attractiveness Stereotype" (Ph.D. diss., University of Pennsylvania, 1975); Arthur Balaskas, *Bodylife* (New York: Grosset and Dunlap, 1977). On the effects of the feminist movement on gender, see Naomi Wolf, *The Beauty Myth: How Images of Beauty Are Used against Women* (New York: William Morrow, 1991), 12–13. On exercise and eating disorders, see Jean Mitchel, "'Going for the Burn' and 'Pumping Iron': What's Healthy about the Current Fitness Boom?" in *Fed Up and Hungry: Women, Oppression, and Food,* ed. M. Lawrence (New York: Peter Bedrick Books, 1987), 156–74; Kathy Peiss, "Making Faces:

The Cosmetic Industry and the Cultural Construction of Gender, 1890–1930," *Genders* 7 (1990): 143–69; Hilde Bruch, *Eating Disorders: Obesity, Anorexia Nervosa, and the Person Within* (New York: Doubleday, 1973); Susan Bordo, "Anorexia Nervosa: Psychopathology as Crystallization of Culture," *Philosophical Forum* 17 (1985–86): 73–103; Kim Chernin, *The Hungry Self: Women, Eating, and Identity* (New York: Times Books, 1985); Katherine Gilday, dir., *The Famine Within* (Ontario: Kandor Productions, 1990).

On gender, appearance, and culture, see Carolyn Heilbrun, *Writing a Woman's Life* (London: Women's Press, 1989), 54; Valerie Steele, *Fashion and Eroticism: Ideals of Feminine Beauty from the Victorian Era to the Jazz Age* (New York: Oxford University Press, 1985); Rita Freedman, *Beauty Bound* (Lexington, Mass.: D.C. Heath, 1986), 2; Susie Orbach, *Fat Is a Feminist Issue: The Anti-Diet Guide to Permanent Weight Loss* (New York: Paddington, 1978); Susie Orbach, *Hunger Strike* (New York: Norton, 1986); Wendy Chapkis, *Beauty Secrets: Women and the Politics of Appearance* (Boston: South End Press, 1986); Barry Glassner, *Bodies: Why We Look the Way We Do (and How We Feel about It)* (New York: G.P. Putnam's Sons, 1988); Sandra Bartkey, *Femininity and Domination: Studies in the Phenomenology of Oppression* (New York: Routledge, 1990); Susan Bordo, "'Material Girl': The Effacements of Postmodern Culture," *Michigan Quarterly Review* 29 (1990): 653–77; Jane Gaines, "Introduction: Fabricating the Female Body," in *Fabrications: Costume and the Female Body,* ed. J. Gaines and C. Herzog (New York: Routledge, 1990), 1–9; Carole Spitzack, *Confessing Excess: Women and the Politics of Body Reduction* (Albany: State University of New York Press, 1990); Natalie Beausoleil, "Makeup in Everyday Life," in Sault, *Many Mirrors,* 33–57; and Margaret Morse, "Artemis Aging: Exercise and the Female Body on Video," *Discourse* 10 (1987–88): 20–53.

5. See Bryan Turner, *The Body and Society: Explorations in Social Theory* (Oxford: Blackwell, 1984); and Elaine Hatfield and Susan Sprecher, *Mirror, Mirror: The Importance of Looks in Everyday Life* (Albany: State University of New York Press, 1986).

6. See Peiss, *Hope in a Jar;* Martin, *Woman in the Body;* Wolf, *Beauty Myth.*

7. Gilday, *Famine Within.*

8. Ibid.

9. C. Wright Mills, "Situated Actions and Vocabularies of Motive," *American Sociological Review* 5 (1940): 904–93.

10. Peter M. Hall and John P. Hewitt, "The Quasi-theory of Communication and the Management of Dissent," *Social Problems* 18 (1970): 17–27; John P. Hewitt and Peter M. Hall, "Social Problems, Problematic Situations, and Quasi-theories," *American Journal of Sociology* 38 (1973): 367–74; Gresham Sykes and David Matza, "Techniques of Neutralization: A Theory of Delinquency," *American Sociological Review* 22 (1957): 664–70.

11. See Fred Davis, "Deviance Disavowal: The Management of Strained Interaction by the Visibly Handicapped," in *The Other Side: Perspectives on Deviance,* ed. H. S. Becker (New York: Free Press, 1964), 119–37; Diana Scully and Joseph Marolla, "Convicted Rapists' Vocabularies of Motive: Excuses and Justifications," *Social Problems* 31 (1985): 530–44; Charles McCaghy, "Child Molesters: A Study of Their Careers as Deviants," in *Criminal Behavior System: A Typology,* ed. M. B. Clinard and R. Quinney (New York: Holt, Rinehart, and Winston, 1967), 75–88; Charles McCaghy, "Drinking and Deviance Disavowal: The Case of Child Molesters," *Social Problems* 16 (1968): 43–49; Scott A. Reid, "Does Exotic Dancing Pay Well But Cost Dearly?" in *Readings in Deviant Behavior,* ed. A. Thio and T. Calhoun (New York: HarperCollins, 1995), 284–88; Ken Levi, "Becoming a Hit Man: Neutralization in a Very Deviant Career," *Urban Life* 10 (1981): 47–63; and Naomi Gerstel, "Divorce and Stigma," *Social Problems* 34 (1987): 172–86.

12. Marvin Scott and Stanford Lyman, "Accounts," *American Sociological Review* 33 (1968): 46–62.

13. John P. Hewitt and Randall Stokes, "Disclaimers," *American Sociological Review* 40 (1975): 3, 6.

14. Ibid., 7.

15. Levi, "Becoming a Hit Man," 47–63; Michael L. Benson, "Denying the Guilty Mind: Accounting for Involvement in a White-Collar Crime," *Criminology* 23 (1985): 589–99.

16. These assertions are based on a large and complex literature dealing with the construction of discourse and its influence on human behaviors and attitudes. Among the works I draw from are Michel Foucault, *The History of Sexuality,* trans. R. Hurley (New York: Pantheon Books, 1981); Pierre Bourdieu, *Distinction: A Social Critique of the Judgment of Taste,* trans. R. Nice (Cambridge: Harvard University Press, 1984); Susan Bordo, "Reading the Slender Body," in *Body/Politics: Women and the Discourses of Science,* ed. M. Jacobus, E. Fox Keller, and S. Shuttleworth (New York: Routledge, 1990), 83–112 (on culture), Rosalind Coward, *Female Desires: How They Are Sought, Bought, and Packaged* (New York: Grove Press, 1985) (on female desire and sexuality), Arleen B. Dallery, "The Politics of Writing (The) Body: Écriture Feminine," in Jaggar and Bordo, *Gender/Body/Knowledge* (on the female body), Judith Fryer, "'The Body in Pain' in Thomas Eakins' *Agnew Clinic*," in *The Female Body: Figures, Styles, Speculations,* ed. L. Goldstein (Ann Arbor: University of Michigan Press, 1991), 235–45 (on nineteenth century painting), Molly Hite, "Writing and Reading the Body: Female Sexuality and Recent Feminist Fiction," *Feminist Studies* 14 (1988): 121–42 (on modern fiction), and Laurie Schulze, "On the Muscle" in Gaines and Herzog, *Fabrications,* 59–78 (on female bodybuilding).

17. As with discourse analysis, symbolic interactionism involves a massive and complicated literature that has considerably influenced work in sociology and social psychology. See George Herbert Mead, *Mind, Self, and Society from the Standpoint of a Social Behaviorist,* ed. C. W. Morris (Chicago: University of Chicago Press, 1934); Erving Goffman, *The Presentation of Self in Everyday Life* (New York: Doubleday, 1959); and Charles Gordon and Kenneth Gergen, eds., *The Self in Social Interaction* (New York: John Wiley, 1968). Very little work in this field has attended to the relationship between the body and the self (for one exception, see Raymond L. Schmidt, "Embodied Identities: Breasts

as Emotional Reminders," *Studies in Symbolic Interactionism* 7 [1986]: 229–89).

18. For other feminist interpretations of the social body, see Marlene Boskind-Lodahl, "Cinderella's Stepsisters: A Feminist Perspective on Anorexia Nervosa and Bulimia," *Signs: Journal of Women, Culture, and Society* 2 (1976): 342–56; Beverly Brown and Parveen Adams, "The Feminine Body and Feminist Politics," *m/f* 3 (1979): 39–50; Carole Counihan, "What Does It Mean to Be Fat, Thin, and Female in the United States? A Review Essay," *Food and Foodways* 1 (1985): 77–94; Diane Barthel, *Putting on Appearances* (Philadelphia: Temple University Press, 1988); Roberta Pollack-Seid, *Never Too Thin: Why Women Are at War with Their Bodies* (New York: Prentice-Hall, 1989); Leslie Heywood, *Dedication to Hunger: The Anorexic Aesthetic in Modern Culture* (Berkeley: University of California Press, 1996); Anne Balsamo, *Technologies of the Gendered Body: Reading Cyborg Women* (Durham, N.C.: Duke University Press, 1996).

19. Michel Foucault, "History of Sexuality," in *Power/Knowledge: Selected Interviews and Other Writings by Michel Foucault, 1972–1977,* trans. and ed. C. Gordon et al. (New York: Pantheon Books, 1980), 186.

20. Scott and Lyman, "Accounts," 46.

CHAPTER 1. THE HAIR SALON

1. See Katherine Perutz, *Beyond the Looking Glass: Life in the Beauty Culture* (New York: Penguin, 1970); Robin Tolmach Lakoff and Raquel L. Scherr, *Face Value: The Politics of Beauty* (Boston: Routledge and Kegan Paul, 1984); Nancy C. Baker, *The Beauty Trap* (New York: Franklin Watts, 1984); Susie Orbach, *Hunger Strike* (New York: Norton, 1986); Rita Freedman, *Beauty Bound* (Lexington, Mass.: D.C. Heath, 1986); Andrea Dworkin, *Woman Hating* (New York: Dutton, 1974), 167–79; and Susie Orbach, *Fat Is a Feminist Issue: The Anti-Diet Guide to Permanent Weight Loss* (New York: Paddington, 1978). For exceptions, see Carole Spitzack, *Confessing Excess: Women and the Politics of Body Reduction* (Albany: State University of New York Press, 1990);

Kathy Davis, *Reshaping the Female Body: The Dilemma of Cosmetic Surgery* (New York: Routledge, 1995). For a discussion of beauty ideals as a backlash against progress attained by the feminist movement, see Naomi Wolf, *The Beauty Myth: How Images of Beauty Are Used against Women* (New York: William Morrow, 1991) 10–12.

2. Gresham Sykes and David Matza, "Techniques of Neutralization: A Theory of Delinquency," *American Sociological Review* 22 (1957): 666.

3. Arlie R. Hochschild, *The Managed Heart: The Commercialization of Human Feeling* (Berkeley: University of California Press, 1983); Robin Leidner, *Fast Food, Fast Talk* (Berkeley: University of California Press, 1993).

4. Lois W. Banner, *American Beauty* (Chicago: University of Chicago Press, 1983), 44.

5. Michelle A. Eayrs, "Time, Trust, and Hazard: Hairdressers' Symbolic Roles," *Symbolic Interaction* 16 (1993): 19–37.

6. Freedman, *Beauty Bound.*

7. *The Sociology of Georg Simmel,* trans. and ed. Kurt H. Wolff (Glencoe, Ill.: Free Press, 1950), 339.

8. Katherine Perutz, *Beyond the Looking Glass: Life in the Beauty Culture* (New York: Penguin, 1970); Anthony Synnot, *The Body Social: Symbolism, Self, and Society* (London: Routledge, 1993).

9. Wolf, *Beauty Myth.*

10. I do not mean to imply that race is unimportant to women's negotiation of the relationship of body and self. In fact, hair appears to be central to many African Americans' identification of self, social class, and community. See Kobena Mercer, *Welcome to the Jungle: New Positions in Black Cultural Studies* (New York: Routledge, 1994); bell hooks, *Black Looks* (Boston: South End Press, 1992); and Kathy Peiss, *Hope in a Jar* (New York: Metropolitan Books, 1998).

11. Margaret King, "The Theme Park Experience: What Museums Can Learn from Mickey," *The Futurist* 25 (1991): 24–31.

12. Wolf, *Beauty Myth;* Baker, *Beauty Trap.*

13. Hochschild, *Managed Heart,* 165.

14. Eayrs, "Time, Trust, and Hazard," 31.

15. David Schroder, *Engagement in the Mirror: Hairdressers and Their Work* (San Francisco: R & E Research Associates, 1978); see also Henri Peretz, "Negotiating Clothing Identities on the Sales Floor," *Symbolic Interaction* 18 (1995): 19–38, for similar findings concerning clothing salespeople.

16. Amy S. Wharton, "The Affective Consequences of Service Work: Managing Emotions on the Job," *Work and Occupations* 20 (1993): 205–32; Martin O'Brien, "The Managed Heart Revisited: Health and Social Control," *Sociological Review* 42 (1994): 393–413.

17. Eayrs, "Time, Trust, and Hazard," 34–37.

18. See also Emory Cowan, "Hairdressers as Caregivers," *American Journal of Community Psychology* 7 (1979): 633–48; Alan Wiesenfeld and Herbert M. Weis, "Hairdressers and Helping: Influencing the Behavior of Informal Caregivers," *Professional Psychology*, (December 1979): 786–92.

19. Hochschild, *Managed Heart,* 181.

CHAPTER 2. AEROBICS

1. Gresham Sykes and David Matza, "Techniques of Neutralization: A Theory of Delinquency," *American Sociological Review* 22 (1957): 664–70; Charles McCaghy, "Child Molesters: A Study of Their Careers as Deviants," in *Criminal Behavior System: A Typology,* ed. M. B. Clinard and R. Quinney (New York: Holt, Rhinehart, and Winston, 1967), 75–88; John P. Hewitt and Randall Stokes, "Disclaimers," *American Sociological Review* 40 (1975): 1–11.

2. Mary Wollstonecraft, *A Vindication of the Rights of Women: With Strictures on Political and Moral Subjects* (London: J. Johnson, 1792); Helen Lenskyj, *Out of Bounds: Women, Sport, and Sexuality* (Toronto: Women's Press, 1986), 11; Sarah Gilroy, "The Embodiment of Power: Gender and Physical Activity," *Leisure Studies* 8 (1989): 163–71; Jen-

nifer Hargreaves, *Sporting Females: Critical Issues in the History and Sociology of Women's Sports* (London: Routledge, 1994), 40; Susan K. Cahn, *Coming On Strong: Gender and Sexuality in Twentieth-Century Women's Sport* (Cambridge: Harvard University Press, 1995).

3. Ruth Colker and Cathy Widom, "Correlates of Female Athletic Participation: Masculinity, Femininity, Self-Esteem, and Attitudes toward Women," *Sex Roles* 6 (1980): 47–58; Rod Beamish, "Materialism and the Comprehension of Gender-Related Issues in Sport," in *Sport and the Sociological Imagination,* refereed proceedings of the Third Annual Conference of the North American Society for the Sociology of Sport, Toronto, Ontario, ed. N. Theberge and P. Donnelly (Fort Worth: Texas Christian University Press, 1986); Diane Hayes and Catherine E. Ross, "Body and Mind: The Effects of Exercise, Overweight, and Physical Health on Psychological Well-Being," *Journal of Health and Social Behavior* 27 (1986): 387–400.

4. Susan Armitage, "The Lady as Jock: A Popular Culture Perspective of the Woman Athlete," *Journal of Popular Culture* 10 (1976): 122–32; Mabel Lee, *Memories beyond Bloomers* (Washington, D.C.: American Alliance for Health, Physical Education, and Recreation, 1978); Bonnie Beck, "The Future of Women's Sports: Issues, Insights, and Struggles," in *Jocks: Sports and Male Identity,* ed. D. Sabo and R. Runfola (Englewood Cliffs, N.J.: Prentice-Hall, 1980), 299–314 ; Bonnie Parkhouse and Jackie Lapin, *Women Who Win* (Englewood Cliffs, N.J.: Prentice-Hall, 1980); David Butt and Marvin Schroeder, "Sex-Role Adaptation, Socialization, and Sport Participation in Women," *International Review of Sport Sociology* 15 (1980): 91–99; Kathleen McCrone, *Sport and the Physical Emancipation of English Women* (London: Routledge, 1988); John Phillips, *Sociology of Sport* (Boston: Allyn and Bacon, 1993).

5. John Leigh, *Young People and Leisure* (London: Routledge and Kegan Paul, 1971).

6. For a review of research on the relationship between gender and sports/recreation, see David H. Smith and Nancy Theberge, *Why People Recreate: An Overview of Research* (Champaign, Ill.: Life Enhance-

ment Publications, 1987), 31–33. See also Canadian Fitness Survey, *Fitness and Lifestyle in Canada* (Ottawa: Canadian Fitness Survey, 1983).

7. Kenneth H. Cooper, *Aerobics* (New York: M. Evans and Company, 1968).

8. Bordo, "Reading the Slender Body," 85.

9. Hargreaves, *Sporting Females,* 160.

10. Morse, "Artemis Aging," 34.

11. Michael Featherstone, "The Body in Consumer Culture," in *The Body: Social Process and Cultural Theory,* ed. M. Featherstone, M. Hepworth, and B. Turner (London: Sage, 1991), 170–96; Joan Finkelstein, *The Fashioned Self* (Philadelphia: Temple University Press, 1991). See also Jean Mitchel, "'Going for the Burn' and 'Pumping Iron': What's Healthy about the Current Fitness Boom?" in *Fed Up and Hungry: Women, Oppression, and Food,* ed. M. Lawrence (New York: Peter Bedrick Books, 1987), 170–74.

12. Featherstone, "The Body in Consumer Culture," 177.

13. Ibid., 190.

14. Ann Swidler, "Culture in Action: Symbols and Strategies," *American Sociological Review* 51 (1986): 273–86.

15. Wendy Chapkis, *Beauty Secrets: Women and the Politics of Appearance* (Boston: South End Press, 1986).

16. Susan Bordo, "Reading the Slender Body," in *Body/Politics: Women and the Discourses of Science,* ed. M. Jacobus, E. Fox Keller, and S. Shuttleworth (New York: Routledge, 1990), 83–112.

17. Ibid.

18. Morse, "Artemis Aging," 34.

19. Featherstone, "The Body in Consumer Culture," 182.

20. Hargreaves, *Sporting Females,* 247.

21. Morse, "Artemis Aging," 35.

CHAPTER 3. COSMETIC SURGERY

1. Ann Dally, *Women under the Knife: A History of Surgery* (London: Hutchinson Radius, 1991); Eugenia Kaw, "Opening Faces: The Poli-

tics of Cosmetic Surgery and Asian-American Women," in *Many Mirrors: Body Image and Social Relations,* ed. N. Sault (New Brunswick, N.J.: Rutgers University Press, 1994), 241–65.

2. American Society of Plastic and Reconstructive Surgeons, *1999 Plastic Surgery Procedural Statistics* (Arlington Heights, Ill.: American Society of Plastic and Reconstructive Surgeons,www.plasticsurgery.org, March 2000); American Society of Plastic and Reconstructive Surgeons, *1999 Average Surgeon's Fees* (Arlington Heights, Ill.: American Society of Plastic and Reconstructive Surgeons, www.plasticsurgery.org., March 2000). Generally, surgeons' fees do not include anesthesia, operating-room facilities, or other related expenses.

3. American Society of Plastic and Reconstructive Surgeons, *1999 Gender Distribution: Cosmetic Procedures* (Arlington Heights, Ill.: American Society of Plastic and Reconstructive Surgeons, www.plastic surgery.org., March 2000).

4. American Society of Plastic and Reconstructive Surgeons, *1999 Plastic Surgery Procedural Statistics* (Arlington Heights, Ill.: www. plasticsurgery.org, March 2000).

5. Joachim Gabka and Ekkchard Vaubel, *Plastic Surgery Past and Present: Origin and History of Modern Lines of Incision* (Basle: Karger, 1983), 29.

6. Susan Faludi, *Backlash: The Undeclared War on Women* (New York: Crown, 1991), 217.

7. Kathy Davis, *Reshaping the Female Body: The Dilemma of Cosmetic Surgery* (New York: Routledge, 1995), 21.

8. Robert M. Goldwyn, ed., *Long-Term Results in Plastic and Reconstructive Surgery,* 2d ed. (Boston: Little, Brown, 1980).

9. Barbara Meredith, *A Change for the Better* (London: Grafton Books, 1988).

10. Susan Bordo, "'Material Girl': The Effacements of Postmodern Culture," *Michigan Quarterly Review* 29 (1990): 657.

11. Joan Finkelstein, *The Fashioned Self* (Philadelphia: Temple University Press, 1991), 87.

12. Naomi Wolf, *The Beauty Myth: How Images of Beauty Are Used against Women* (New York: William Morrow, 1991).

13. See Davis, *Reshaping the Female Body,* for similar findings.

14. Concern about authenticity may well be class-specific; however, because my sample is based on references from a plastic surgeon, it is likely to include those patients who are least troubled by what they have done.

CHAPTER 4. NAAFA

1. NAAFA home page, "General Information," www.NAAFA.org, March 2001.

2. Ibid.

3. Gresham Sykes and David Matza, "Techniques of Neutralization: A Theory of Delinquency," *American Sociological Review* 22 (1957): 669.

4. To protect the anonymity of study participants, I created "Sylvia" as a composite of several members of NAAFA.

5. Erving Goffman, *The Presentation of Self in Everyday Life* (New York: Doubleday Anchor, 1959), 111.

6. Ibid., 108.

7. NAAFA Workbook Committee, *NAAFA Workbook: A Complete Study Guide* (Sacramento: NAAFA, 1993), chapter 8.

8. Albert J. Stunkard, "Genetic Factors in Obesity," *New England Journal of Medicine* 314 (1986): 192–98.

9. NAAFA Workbook Committee, *NAAFA Workbook,* 8.5.

10. Ibid., 8.6.

11. Ibid., 8.7.

12. Goffman, *Presentation of Self,* 108.

13. NAAFA Workbook Committee, *NAAFA Workbook,* 6.6.

14. Ibid., 6.4.

15. Ibid., 2.6.

16. Ibid., 2.5.

17. Ibid., 1.5.

18. Ibid., 6.7.

19. Marcia Millman, *Such a Pretty Face: Being Fat in America* (New York: Norton, 1980).

20. NAAFA Workbook Committee, *NAAFA Workbook,* chapter 5.

21. Ibid.

22. Harold Garfinkel, *Studies in Ethnomethodology* (Englewood Cliffs, N.J.: Prentice-Hall, 1967).

23. Michael L. Benson, "Denying the Guilty Mind: Accounting for Involvement in a White-Collar Crime," *Criminology* 23 (1985): 589–99.

24. Ibid., 589.

25. Naomi Gerstel, "Divorce and Stigma," *Social Problems* 34 (1987): 183.

26. Ibid., 182.

27. Ibid., 184.

28. Ken Levi, "Becoming a Hit Man: Neutralization in a Very Deviant Career," *Urban Life* 10 (1981): 47–63.

CONCLUSION

1. Margaret Morse, "Artemis Aging: Exercise and the Female Body on Video," *Discourse* 10 (1987–88): 20–53.

INDEX

Aerobics: as denial of responsibility for appearance, 50, 56–65; as distinguished from sports, 52; emphasis on character over appearance, 56, 62, 63, 65, 145; feminist views on, 52, 67–68, 69, 70, 72; to gain sense of control over one's body, 65; group culture aspects of, 65–66, 69–70, 108–9, 147; narcissism and competition in, 69–70; popularity of, 51–52; to reduce stigma of flawed body, 65, 71; to renegotiate meanings of body and self, 51, 52, 56, 60–62, 63, 65, 71, 72, 145; and self-confidence, 68–69, 71; and self-discipline, 13, 56, 61–62

Aerobics classes: concerns about skipping, 61–62, 148; focus on "trouble spots," 144; mirrors in, 53, 144; research settings and subjects, 11–12, 52–56; social aspects of, 66, 69, 70–71

African American women, 21, 157n10

Age discrimination: as motivation for having plastic surgery, 89

Appearance. *See* Beauty ideals; Physical appearance

Asian women: eye-reshaping procedures and, 79, 99

Athletics: aerobics as distinct from sports, 52; confidence and empowerment from, 51, 66; feminist views on female participation in, 51, 52; gender differences in, 51–52

Baker, Nancy, 27

Beauticians. *See* Hairstylists

Beauty ideals: alternative, aerobics as social context for, 65, 66, 67, 68; as backlash against women's social and economic gains, 16; beauty industry and, 17, 47, 75; as essence of femininity, 26; ethnic aspects of, 79, 99–100, 142; idealization of youth,

Motivations for cosmetic surgery
(*continued*)
to reduce markers of ethnicity, 79,
99, 142; to reduce signs of aging,
89, 98–99

NAAFA (National Association to
Advance Fat Acceptance), 9,
10–11, 122–23; attitudes toward
thin women, 113–14; body-self
relationship conceptualizations,
123; as civil rights organization,
111, 115, 127; goals of, 111; group
culture aspects of, 108–9, 147; history of, 111; and job strategies for
members, 128; members' weight
loss attempts, 118, 136–37;
normative identity and, 112–13,
140, 148; research settings and
subjects, 113–22; sexualization of
fat, 133, 134–35, 144; social
events, 2, 111–12, 132–33; as welcoming social environment,
118–19, 120. *See also* Fat Feminist
Caucus; Fat women; Obesity
Norm violation: success of attempts
to neutralize, 139–40. *See also*
Deviance; Linguistic accounts
Norris, John, M.D. (plastic surgeon),
1, 81–86, 88, 93, 142; patient selec-
tion criteria, 83–85; personality
and background, 82–83
Nose job. *See* Rhinoplasty

Obesity: as accident of nature, 124,
130; cultural stigmatization of,
111, 135, 139, 140. *See also* Fat
women; NAAFA; Physical
appearance

Pamela's Hair Salon: as research
setting, 9, 13, 20–24
Patients. *See* Cosmetic surgery
patients
Personality: physical appearance as
indicator of, 80, 95, 104. *See also
under specific types of body work*
Physical appearance: as accident of
nature, aerobics and, 51, 58, 145;
as accident of nature, cosmetic
surgery and, 80, 95, 96, 107, 146;
as accident of nature, obesity and,
124, 130; age discrimination and,
89; average body size, increase of,
5; as character indicator, 5, 15, 64,
80, 95, 104, 106, 111, 124; family
criticism of, 59–60, 117–18,
119–20; male criticism of, 58–59,
122; self-control over, 65, 96; self-
image and, 57, 94; self-perception
of, as altered by transformative
experiences, 57–59; "trouble
spots," 144. *See also* Beauty ideals;
Ideal body; Obesity
Physicians. *See* Cosmetic surgeons
Plastic surgeons. *See* Cosmetic
surgeons
Plastic surgery, 10, 76; aesthetic operations, prevalence of, 76; fees
for, 75, 161n2; gender of patients,
75. *See also* Cosmetic surgery

Rhinoplasty (nose job): case example,
96–97; ethnicity and, 79, 99, 142

Scott, Marvin, 6
Self-discipline: aerobics and,
13, 56, 61–62; lapses in,
61, 64

Compositor:	Impressions Book and Journal Services, Inc.
Text:	11/15 Granjon
Display:	Granjon
Printer/Binder:	Haddon Craftsmen, Inc.